Access and Engagement

**Program Design and Instructional Approaches
for Immigrant Students in Secondary School**

Printed in the United States of America
10 9 8 7 6 5 4 3 2 1

Topics in Immigrant Education 4
Language in Education: Theory and Practice 94

Editorial/production supervision: Joy Kreeft Peyton and Sonia Kundert
Editorial assistance: Adriana Vaznaugh
Copyediting: Lynn Fischer and Sonia Kundert
Production: Sonia Kundert
Indexing: Kathleen McLane
Design and cover: SAGARTdesign

ISBN 1-887744-09-6

The writing and production of this volume were supported in part by a grant from the Andrew W. Mellon Foundation, as one aspect of the Program in Immigrant Education, and in part by the U.S. Department of Education, Office of Educational Research and Improvement, National Library of Education, under contract No. ED-99-CO-0008. The opinions expressed in this report do not necessarily reflect the positions or policies of the Andrew W. Mellon Foundation or the Department of Education.

Library of Congress Cataloging-in-Publication Data
Walqui, Aída, 1947-
    Access and engagement : program design and instructional approaches for immigrant students in secondary school / Aída Walqui.
       p. cm. -- (Topics in immigrant education ; 4) (Language in education ; 94)
    Includes bibliographical references (p.) and index.
    ISBN 1-887744-09-06 (pbk.)
       1. Children of immigrants--Education (Secondary)--United States--Case studies. 2. Education, Secondary--United States--Curricula. I. Title. II. Series. III. Series: Language in education ; 94
LC3746 .W25 2000
373.1826'91'0973--dc21   99-057258

Access and Engagement

Program Design and Instructional Approaches for Immigrant Students in Secondary School

Aída Walqui
University of California, Santa Cruz

 Delta Systems Co., Inc. CAL ERIC®

Topics in Immigrant Education Series

Series Editors:
Joy Kreeft Peyton and Donna Christian
Center for Applied Linguistics
Washington DC

Into, Through, and Beyond Secondary School:
Critical Transitions for Immigrant Youths
by Tamara Lucas
ISBN 1-887744-03-7

New Concepts for New Challenges:
Professional Development for Teachers of Immigrant Youth
by Josué M. González & Linda Darling-Hammond
ISBN 1-887744-04-5

Through the Golden Door:
Educational Approaches for Immigrant Adolescents With Limited
Schooling
by Betty J. Mace-Matluck, Rosalind Alexander-Kasparik,
& Robin M. Queen
ISBN 1-887744-07-X

Access and Engagement:
Program Design and Instructional Approaches for Immigrant
Students in Secondary School
by Aída Walqui
ISBN 1-887744-09-6

LIST OF TABLES AND FIGURES

After a hiatus of half a century, a wave of immigration is once again transforming the United States. With over a million immigrants, legal and illegal, entering the United States each year, the foreign born constitute the fastest-growing segment of our population, reaching 25.8 million in 1997, roughly 10% of the population, the highest proportion since World War II (U.S. Bureau of the Census, 1997a).

Even more striking than the scale of immigration is its makeup. Since the passage of the Immigration Act of 1965, which eliminated national origin quotas, Asia and Latin America have replaced Europe as the main sources of newcomers to the United States. The largest groups come from Mexico, China, Cuba, India, and Vietnam.

New immigrants to the United States come with diverse languages, cultures, and experiences, even within these larger groups. Asian immigrants, for example, include people from more than 13 countries in South, Southeast, and East Asia as well as the Pacific Islands. A single nationality can include several ethnic groups, each with a distinctive language and culture. A Laotian immigrant might be an ethnic Lao or a member of the Hmong, Mien, or Khmu ethnic minorities. An Asian Indian immigrant might be a Punjabi-speaking Sikh, a Bengali-speaking Hindu, or an Urdu-speaking Moslem.

While the great majority of Latin American immigrants share a common language, and to some extent a common culture, this group also displays a great diversity that is due to the various ancestries—European, African, and Native American—and nations represented. Recent Latin American immigrants have arrived chiefly from Mexico, El Salvador, Guatemala, Nicaragua, and Honduras. Caribbeans, arriving in smaller numbers, come mostly from Haiti, the Dominican Republic, Jamaica, and Cuba.

Today's immigrants also vary in their social and educational backgrounds and personal experiences. They come from the elite as well as the most disadvantaged sectors of their societies. Some left their countries to escape poverty; others were fleeing war or political persecution;

others were attracted by the hope for better educational and economic opportunities. Some came directly to the United States; others arrived after harrowing escapes followed by years in refugee camps.

Immigrant Students in America's Schools

While immigration has affected all aspects of American life, nowhere is the changing demography of the United States more keenly felt than in education. First- and second-generation immigrant children are the fastest-growing segment of the U.S. population under age 15. In the fall of 1997, 9 million (about one in five) elementary and secondary school students had a foreign-born parent. If current trends continue, children of immigrants will account for 88 % of the increase in the under-18 population between 2000 and 2050 (U. S. Bureau of the Census, 1997b).

With over 90% of recent immigrants coming from non-English-speaking countries, schools are increasingly receiving students who do not speak English at home and who have little or no proficiency in English. It is difficult to determine the number of English language learners who are considered limited English proficient (LEP, the term used by the federal government and most states), because states determine numbers of LEP students in different ways (Gándara, 1994; Waggoner, 1999). However, the Office of Bilingual Education and Minority Languages Affairs of the U.S. Department of Education reported 3.2 million LEP students nationwide in 1998, a number that has nearly doubled in less than a decade (U.S. Department of Education, 1998). The largest proportion of this population (roughly 73%) are native Spanish speakers. California has been particularly affected. The number of students classified as LEP in the state's public schools more than tripled from nearly 400,000 in 1981 to nearly 1.4 million in 1997. These students were reported to speak one or more of 54 different primary languages.

Along with an increase in sheer numbers of immigrant students who are at various stages of learning English, schools are also faced with an increasing number of students needing extra academic instruction in addition to English as a second language (ESL) classes. Numbers vary from district to district, but already at the beginning of the 1990s approximately 20% of English language learners at the high school level and 12% at the middle school level had missed 2 or more years of schooling since the age of six; 27% in high school and 19% in middle school were assigned to grades at least 2 years lower than age/grade norms (Fleischman & Hopstock, 1993; see also Short, 1998, for discussion).

Newcomers to this country settle primarily in certain areas, so that the majority of LEP students in K-12 public schools have lived in only five states—California, Florida, Illinois, New York, and Texas (82% in 1993-94, with more than 40% in California; NCES, 1996b). Dade County, Florida, is one such school system, struggling to serve a sudden influx of immigrants. Approximately one quarter of the 330,000 students in Dade County in Fall 1996 were born outside the United States (Schnaiberg, 1996), and the county adds an average of 1,322 foreign-born students a month to its rolls. At the same time, employment opportunities and social connections are drawing immigrants to smaller cities and rural areas as well, so that the number of LEP students is increasing in school systems across the country. For example, between the 1990-91 and 1994-95 school years, the LEP student population in Arkansas increased by 120%; in Kansas by 118%; and in Wisconsin, by 92%(NCES, 1997). Current projections indicate that by the year 2000, the majority of the school-age population in 50 or more major U.S. cities will be from language minority backgrounds (Council of Chief State School Officers, 1998). These patterns create new challenges for schools in those areas.

An increasingly diverse student population is entering U.S. schools at the same time as a record number of students in general are entering school (the *baby boom echo* and the *Millennium Generation,* terms used by demographers to refer to children of the original baby boomers; see Russakoff, 1998). In the Fall of 1999, 53.2 million elementary and secondary school students entered school, setting a new national enrollment record for the fourth year in a row, according to the U.S. Department of Education (1999). The Department predicts that we are in the midst of a "long, slow, rising wave" of school enrollment that shows no sign of stopping. The greatest increase over the next decade will be in high school enrollments, projected to increase by 9% between 1999 and 2009 (from 1.4 million in 1999 to 16.2 million in 2009). Thus, schools already struggling with the influx of immigrant students are also facing the strains of high overall enrollments.

Understanding the Immigrant Student Population

In this series, the term "immigrant" includes those students (including refugees) born outside the United States, but not those born and raised in non-English speaking homes within the United States. Within this group, the focus is on English language learners who are in ESL or bilingual classes, those who no longer have access to ESL or bilingual services but are having trouble in academic classes taught in English, and those who are literate in their native language as well as those who are not. Because the series focuses on students for whom secondary school is a reasonable placement, students' ages range from 9 to 21 years.

U.S.-born students enter school at age 5 or 6 and, if they remain in school, follow a fairly predictable sequence of coursework as they progress to secondary school. Educators can, therefore, assume certain experiences and knowledge among those students. However, no such assumptions can be made about adolescent immigrant students' educational backgrounds and readiness for secondary schooling in the United States. Immigrant students arrive at all ages. They may have had an educational preparation superior to that provided by most U.S. schools, or they may have had no previous educational experience at all. Thus, different educational approaches are called for with these students—for example, a 15-year-old who immigrated from Mexico at age 13 with a strong educational background, one who immigrated at age 13 with only 2 years of prior schooling, and one who immigrated at age 7 and entered school immediately.

Many additional factors can affect immigrant students' adjustment to U.S. schooling and their success in the transition from adolescence to adulthood. These include individual and family characteristics (including socioeconomic status and previous academic achievement), language proficiencies (both native language and English), the similarities and differences between their native countries and cultures and the United States, their immigration experiences and status, and the contexts in which they live in the United States. (See chapter 1 of this volume and chapter 5 of Lucas's [1997] volume in this series for more extensive discussion.) Knowledge of these factors can form the foundation upon which educators build programs and approaches that will assist these students in making their way through school and on to postsecondary school or work.

Facing the Challenges

The demographic realities described above are cause for serious concern, and many educators believe that the education system in the United States is poorly prepared to meet the needs of its linguistically and culturally diverse student population. Gándara (1994) claims that English language learners were sidelined in the first wave of reform efforts during the 1980s, and a report by the Stanford Working Group (1993) calls the nation's school systems to task for failing to provide these students with equitable educational opportunities. Moss and Puma (1995) found that English language learners receive lower grades and are judged by their teachers to have lower academic abilities than native-born students, and they score below their native English-speaking classmates on standardized tests of reading and math.

The challenges of educating immigrant students and English language learners are especially acute at the secondary school level. Immigrant students of secondary school age can face major difficulties in acquiring English and succeeding in school. If they are newcomers to the

United States, they have much less time than elementary age students to learn English and master the academic content required to graduate from high school. They must pass tests that require English skills that they do not have. They must study subjects such as physical science, chemistry, economics, and geometry that require high levels of English academic language. Most secondary school texts and materials require a high level of English reading ability. Many schools still do not provide native-language support for these classes, English-language instruction tied to content, or content classes taught with adaptations of English appropriate for these students' levels of English proficiency. Students learning English often find it difficult to be accepted in well-established groups of English-speaking students. Finally, students who hope to attend college or university after high school face even greater challenges, as they attempt to succeed in classes designated for college credit and to master the maze of requirements for college acceptance.

High dropout rates among language-minority secondary school students are just one indication that many schools are failing to meet the challenge. For example, Hispanic students are more likely than White students to leave school during their high school years (10% versus 4%; National Center for Education Statistics, 1996). In 1994, the number of Hispanic students aged 16-24 who had not completed high school and were not enrolled was 30%, as compared to 8% for White students (Lockwood & Secada, 1999; Secada et al., 1998). Certain subgroups of Asian refugee populations also have high dropout rates. For example, a study of dropout rates in California schools found that those schools with high concentrations of Southeast Asians had the highest dropout rates (U.S. Commission on Civil Rights, 1992).

A number of factors underlie the failure of secondary schools to serve the needs of immigrant students. These include

• a school structure that does not facilitate smooth transitions from program to program, school to school, or school to college or work;

- an instructional program that fails to give English language learners access to academic concepts and skills;
- few program and curricular alternatives for students with limited prior schooling and low literacy skills; and
- a shortage of school personnel trained to meet the specific needs of these groups of students.

These factors characterize an educational system that has failed to keep up with its changing population, particularly at the secondary school level. At the same time, relatively little research is available on effective approaches for educating students at this level (August & Hakuta, 1997).

Books in the Series

The four books in this series (*Topics in Immigrant Education*) address these issues, providing profiles of immigrant students from a variety of backgrounds, critical reviews of what we know from research, and descriptions of challenges that schools face and of programs that show promise. This volume focuses specifically on program features and instructional strategies that are effective in promoting the educational success of immigrant students learning English. The other three focus on promoting students' transitions through and beyond secondary school, innovations in professional development for teachers of immigrant adolescents, and approaches for immigrant adolescents with limited schooling and low literacy skills.

Access and Engagement: Program Design and Instructional Approaches for Immigrant Students in Secondary School, **by Aída Walqui**

In this book, the fourth in this series, Aída Walqui describes characteristics of secondary schools in the United States that make it difficult for immigrant students (and many other students as well) to succeed. These include

- fragmented school days, fragmented instructional programs in which ESL and content area teachers work in separate departments and rarely interact,
- the complex system of courses and of graduation and college entrance requirements,
- the practices of placing students in grades according to their age and of tracking students learning English into courses that may not grant the credits they need, and
- the inadequate methods used to document student achievement.

She profiles six immigrant high school students (from Brazil, El Salvador, Haiti, Mexico, Russia, and Vietnam), their educational backgrounds and language proficiencies, and the challenges they face in school (including students who had strong educational backgrounds before entering school in the United States as well as students with limited prior schooling who are struggling in school).

Walqui addresses common misconceptions about adolescents' second language acquisition and academic needs that drive much instruction in this country and summarizes what we know from research. She describes the philosophies, designs, and instructional approaches of four exemplary programs (in California, Iowa, and New York) attempting to address these challenges. She puts forward 10 priorities for the design of programs that can foster effective teaching and learning for immigrant youth. These include creating a community of learners in the classroom and ensuring that immigrant students are part of the community, contextualizing new ideas and tasks, and giving students multiple (and recursive) opportunities to extend their understandings and apply their knowledge. Finally, she makes recommendations for program development and practice and suggests future directions for research.

Into, Through, and Beyond Secondary School: Critical Transitions for Immigrant Youths, **by Tamara Lucas**

Immigrant adolescents who enter U.S. schools with limited proficiency in English must negotiate a series of critical transitions in order to progress through school. At the same time that they are dealing with the difficult developmental transitions from childhood to adolescence to adulthood, they also must make the transitions from their native country to the United States; from middle school to high school; from bilingual and ESL classes to content area classes; and from high school to postsecondary education or work. In this book, Lucas argues that in order for schools to help immigrant students make these transitions successfully, we must apply the best knowledge we have about teaching, learning, and schooling. We must reconceptualize our notions of learners and learning, teachers and teaching, and schools and schooling. Lucas discusses four specific principles that secondary school staff can apply to facilitate these reconceptualizations and to promote students' transitions—cultivate organizational relationships; provide access to information; cultivate human relationships; and provide multiple and flexible pathways into, through, and beyond secondary school. She provides a set of questions that school staff can use to guide them in establishing effective practices within each principle, and she describes programs in which these principles have been implemented.

New Concepts for New Challenges: Professional Development for Teachers of Immigrant Youth, **by Josué M. González and Linda Darling-Hammond**

Because of immigrant students' diverse backgrounds and needs, school staff need specialized preparation to work effectively with them. All teachers with immigrant students and English language learners in their classes need to know about second language and literacy development, cross-cultural issues, and methods to teach both language and academic content. However, most classroom teachers, counselors, and administrators receive no special training in these areas, and they have limited opportunities to update their knowledge and skills on an ongoing basis. In this book, González and Darling-Hammond describe the challenges to developing a teaching force that is competent to work with immigrant students and develop a framework for considering what teachers of immigrant youth need to understand about their students, what kinds of professional development experiences are likely to facilitate those understandings, and what kinds of teacher education programs and school settings are able to support their ongoing learning. They describe promising new structures and practices for professional development, focusing particularly on those that promote community, collegiality, and collaboration. Finally, they profile innovative approaches to preservice and inservice professional development in California, Maryland, Minnesota, and New York.

Through the Golden Door: Educational Approaches for Immigrant Adolescents With Limited Schooling, **by Betty Mace-Matluck, Rosalind Alexander-Kasparik, and Robin M. Queen**

A growing number of recent immigrant adolescents enter middle school and high school with little or no former schooling and with only basic literacy skills. As a result, they often have difficulty in secondary school and not enough time to fulfill high school graduation requirements before they reach the maximum age for high school attendance. This book summarizes the information available about these students and describes the backgrounds, educational experiences, and needs of five such students from Haiti, El Salvador, and Vietnam. The authors profile four programs (in Illinois, Texas, and Virginia) with innovative structures and instructional strategies designed to meet the needs of these students, identify the critical features of effective programs for them, and discuss areas in which further research is needed.

Conclusion

New visions of learning, teaching, and schooling push us to break through the traditional boundaries of the classroom and the school and to redefine who participates in teaching and learning and in what ways. Immigrant students must be included in the population of all students whom school reform movements and new approaches to schooling are designed to serve. We can no longer develop programs that ignore the needs of these students and deprive them of the benefits of broad educational reforms. The education of immigrant students needs to sit squarely within the educational reform movement, so that those students of secondary school age have access to high-quality programs in school, postsecondary opportunities beyond school, and the opportunity to become productive members of our society.

To do this, we need strong, responsive school programs and instructional practices that provide opportunities for immigrant students to learn academic content while they are learning English, that smooth their transitions through and beyond school, and that are sensitive to the special needs of students with limited prior schooling and low literacy skills. Educators of these students need to understand the principles and practices of educational reform and participate in the design and implementation of new programs and approaches. Finally, all educators must develop culturally and linguistically responsive understandings and skills to facilitate the success of all of their students.

Series Acknowledgments

The Program in Immigrant Education, begun in 1993, was funded by The Andrew W. Mellon Foundation to improve immigrant students' access to high-quality education in secondary school, their success in school, and their transitions to education and work after high school. Demonstration projects in Northern California, Southern California, Maryland, and Texas were established to implement, document, and evaluate innovative projects to accomplish these general goals.

This book series was developed to inform project staff as well as researchers and practitioners working with immigrant students about topics that are critical to this effort. After extensive conversations with project directors and staff, advisors to the program, and leaders in the field of immigrant education, priority topics were identified. For each topic, authors were asked to review what is known, document promising programs, and identify available resources.

We are grateful for the input we received on topics, authors, and book content from project staff Albert Cortez, JoAnn Crandall, Ann Jaramillo, Laurie Olsen, and David Ramírez; program advisors Keith Buchanan, Margarita Calderón, Eugene García, Victoria Jew, Eric Nadelstern, and Delia Pompa; colleagues Michelle Brewer Byrd, Russell Campbell, Rosa Castro Feinberg, Kenji Hakuta, Tamara Lucas, Betty Mace-Matluck, Denise McKeon, and G. Richard Tucker; and CAL staff member Deborah Short. We extend special thanks to Tamara Lucas, who provided information included in the introduction; to Sonia Kundert, who coordinated the books' production; to Lynn Fischer and Amy Fitch, who provided editorial assistance; to Adriana Vaznaugh for collecting information and communicating with authors; and to Vincent Sagart, who designed the book covers and interiors. Finally, we are grateful to Stephanie Bell-Rose and Stephanie Creaturo, program officers at The Andrew W. Mellon Foundation, for their support of the work of the Program in Immigrant Education.

Joy Kreeft Peyton and Donna Christian, Series Editors

References

August, D., & Hakuta, K. (1997). *Improving schooling for language-minority children: A research agenda.* Washington, DC: National Academy Press.

Council of Chief State School Officers. (1998). *State education indicators with a focus on Title I.* Washington, DC: Author

Fleischman, H.L., & Hopstock, P.J. (1993). *Descriptive study of services to limited English proficient students: Vol. 1. Summary of findings and conclusions.* Arlington, VA: Development Associates.

Gándara, P. (1994). The impact of the education reform movement on limited English proficient students. In B. McLeod (Ed.), *Language and learning: Educating linguistically diverse students* (pp. 45-70). Albany, NY: SUNY Press.

Lockwood, A.T., & Secada, W.G. (1999, January). *Transforming education for Hispanic youth: Exemplary practices, programs, and schools* (NCBE Resource Collection Series, No. 12). Available: http://www.ncbe.gwu.edu/ncbepubs/resource/hispanicyouth/index.htm

Moss, M., & Puma, M. (1995). *Prospects: The Congressionally mandated study of educational growth and opportunity.* Cambridge, MA: Abt Associates.

National Center for Education Statistics. (1996). *Dropout rates in the United States: 1994* (NCES 96-863). Washington, DC: U.S. Government Printing Office. Available: http://www.nces.ed.gov/pubsold/r94/index.html

Russakoff, D. (1998, June 29). The 'Millennium Generation' is making its mark. *Washington Post,* pp. A1, A9.

Schnaiberg, L. (1996, September 11). Immigration plays key supporting role in record-enrollment drama. *Education Week, 16,* 24-25.

Secada, W.G., Chavez-Chavez. R., Garcia, E., Muñoz, C., Oakes, J., Santiago-Santiago, I., & Slavin, R. (1998, February). *No more excuses: The final report of the Hispanic dropout project.* Washington, DC: U.S. Department of Education. Available: http://www.ed.gov/offices/OBEMLA/hdprepo.pdf

Short, D.J. (1998, March). *Secondary newcomer programs: Helping recent immigrants prepare for school success. ERIC Digest.* Washington, DC: ERIC Clearinghouse on Languages and Linguistics. Available: http://www.cal.org/ericcll/digest/short001.html

Stanford Working Group. (1993). *Federal education programs for limited-English-proficient students: A blueprint for the second generation.* Stanford, CA: Stanford University.

U.S. Bureau of the Census. (1997a). *The foreign born population: March 1997 (Update)* (P20-507 and PPL-92). Available: http://www.census.gov/population/www/socdemo/foreign97.html

U.S. Bureau of the Census. (1997b). *School enrollment in the United States—Social and economic characteristics of students: October 1997* (P20-516). Available: http://www.census.gov/Press-Release/www/1999/cb99-124.html

U.S. Commission on Civil Rights. (1992, February). *Civil rights issues facing Asian Americans in the 1990s.* Washington, DC: Author.

U.S. Department of Education, Office of Bilingual Education and Minority Languages Affairs. (1998, May 11). *Facts about limited English proficient students.* Washington, DC: Author. Available: http://www.ed.gov/offices/OBLEMA/rileyfct.html

U.S. Department of Education. (1999, August 19). *A back to school special report on the baby boom echo: No end in sight.* Washington, DC: Author. Available: http://www.ed.gov/pubs/bbecho99/part1.html

Waggoner, D. (1999). From the editor. *Numbers and Needs: Ethnic and Linguistic Minorities in the United States, 9*(3), 1. Available: http://asu.edu/educ/cber/n_n/edmay99.htm

This book could not have been written without the contributions of many colleagues, teachers, students, parents, and school administrators. In June 1994 a group of researchers met at Stanford University and helped me brainstorm ideas, suggested directions for the monograph, and proposed candidate sites for the case studies. I would like to thank Kenji Hakuta, Victoria Jew, Guadalupe Valdés, Walter Secada, Delia Pompa, Rosalía Salinas, Mary Cazabon, Tomás Galguera, Deborah Short, Jerome Shaw, and Lydia Stack for those rich and inspiring conversations.

Later I talked with many people around the country on the telephone. Invariably they offered useful information and suggestions. I would especially like to thank Catherine Minicucci, Hugh Mehan, Else Hamayan, and Laurie Olsen. During the days I spent visiting school sites, teachers, students, and administrators generously gave their ideas and their time. Among them I especially want to thank Oscar Fragas of the New Beginnings Program in Dade County, Florida; Caroline Donaway in Sioux City, Iowa; Charlie Glassman, Aaron Listhaus, and David Hirschy at the International High School in New York; Emily Palacio and Gil Mendez in Calexico, California; and Cindy Lenners and Kelly Smith in Salinas, California.

This book also benefited from conversations with and suggestions from Tamara Lucas and Josué González, authors of companion books in the series, as well as from members of the advisory group for the Program in Immigrant Education—Keith Buchanan, Margarita Calderón, Victoria Jew, and Eric Nadelstern. My editor, Joy Peyton, deserves special thanks for the detail and insight with which she has reviewed the various versions of the manuscript.

Comments and criticisms from a number of colleagues from the larger educational community have been very helpful in reconsidering and revising the original draft. These include Laura Woodlief, Leo van Lier, Leslie Hamburger, and Ruth Barraza.

Finally, I thank the Andrew W. Mellon Foundation for having the vision and the commitment to support and become involved in immigrant education and for supporting the writing of this book.

Most research on the education of immigrant students has concentrated on students at the elementary school level. Consequently, we now possess significant knowledge about how to address the needs of English language learners in elementary schools (Carter & Chatfield, 1986; Faltis, 1993; García, 1992, 1994, 1996; Heath, 1983; Olsen & Dowell, 1989; Pease-Alvarez, Espinosa, & García, 1991; Ramírez, Yuen, Ramey, & Pasta, 1991), although widespread implementation of carefully designed programs at this level has still not occurred. However, there is another important population of English language learners in our schools—those who attend secondary schools. Their presence is numerically significant and increasing, yet we know little about them and their needs. This lack of knowledge leaves school systems facing myriad situations they are unprepared to meet. In the rush of school staff to respond, students often suffer irreparable damage.

The number of immigrant teenagers in American schools is increasing continuously. Although California, Florida, Illinois, New Jersey, New York, and Texas have traditionally experienced the greatest impact of foreign migration (McDonnell & Hill, 1993), the presence of immigrant students at the secondary school level has also affected areas of the country that we seldom associate with the recent immigrant influx, such as the Midwest.

There is little doubt that teenage immigrant students present the U.S. educational system with challenges that most schools and teachers are unprepared to meet and for which there are no easy answers. At the same time, these students bring strengths that can benefit everyone, if we learn to capitalize on them. The purpose of this book is to contribute to our knowledge base by reviewing relevant research about these students and by examining effective programs for them. My main premise is that understanding the unique needs of these students is necessary if we are to educate them effectively.

In this volume, I first present the characteristics and needs of immigrant students in secondary schools in the United States and the issues involved in their education. I then describe programs seeking ways to work with them effectively. In chapter 1, I profile six immigrant high school students because we cannot serve these students well unless we know who they are in all their diversity. In chapter 2, I examine second language acquisition among immigrant teenagers, first by focusing on some of the common misconceptions we have about their language learning and academic needs, and then by examining what we currently know about the complex processes of second language acquisition. Because language learning does not take place in a vacuum, I consider some of the major social and cultural contexts of second language development for immigrant and minority students: Chapter 3 focuses on school structures that make it difficult for immigrant students to succeed in school, and chapter 4 focuses on characteristics of effective teaching and learning for the adolescent English language learners in our schools.

After setting the stage from these various perspectives—that of the students themselves, of second language acquisition processes, of social and cultural contexts for learning, and of ineffective and effective educational practices—in chapter 5, I present profiles of four exemplary programs. While these programs form the heart of this book, the larger perspectives of the previous chapters are necessary to appreciate fully how well these programs function. In the concluding chapter, I reflect on these programs and the state of education generally for immigrant teenagers. I offer recommendations for improving educational access and engagement for these students. These recommendations include offering them opportunities to participate in instructional activities and giving them appropriate assistance so that these opportunities are optimized.

This book relies on two sources of information: a review of relevant literature, including research about and written descriptions of programs, and data collected especially for this study during visits to programs selected for their impressive efforts to address the needs of immigrant students.

Understanding the Needs of Immigrant Secondary School Students

Who Are Our Students?

As I visited middle schools and high schools to write this book, I met many bright, energetic, hard-working young men and women. They all shared the immigrant experience and the difficulties of adapting to new ways of saying and doing things. They also shared the dream of contributing to a better future for American society, for their relatives, and for themselves. At the same time, they were all distinct individuals—with different personalities, different native languages, and above all, vastly different reasons for coming to the United States. In an effort to understand the variety of immigrant students in our schools, I have constructed profiles of real students I talked with at length while visiting their schools. Their names and some minor details of their lives have been changed for their protection, but the important aspects of their lives remain intact. These profiles focus on aspects of their backgrounds that are most likely to shape their education in U.S. secondary schools—their previous schooling, English and native language abilities, family and community support systems, immigration status, economic success in the United States, and their own hopes and dreams.

I begin with these students, not simply because they represent a variety of backgrounds and needs, but also because effective programs and instructional approaches must begin with a compassionate understanding of their students. It is tempting, with immigrant students, to focus solely on their linguistic knowledge; however, many of the challenges that they face are not only linguistic, but economic, cultural, academic, and personal as well. By getting to know these students as individuals who nonetheless share similar language, economic, and educational backgrounds, we can build on their strengths and address their needs more effectively.

Profiles of Six Immigrant Students

• **Martín** was born in El Salvador, where he lived for 11 years in a rural area. When Martín was in the third grade, the political situation in his country interrupted his schooling. Martín's father had worked in a large hacienda all his life, but with the war in El Salvador, such work became untenable, and the family decided to move to "El Norte," the United States. Initially his father, accompanied by Martín's older brother, crossed the border and went to Bakersfield, California. There they had relatives working in the fields who could ensure they would have food and a bed until his father found work. Martín, his mother, and his youngest brother followed a year later, after his father had saved enough money to rent an apartment. A month after Martín and his mother arrived, however, flooding in the Central Valley destroyed the crops, and Martín's father, along with many other field workers, lost his job.

The family's relatives in Sioux City, Iowa, who worked in the meat-packing industry, encouraged them to move there. Just when Martín was beginning to find his way in Bakersfield, the family packed what could fit into their blue and white 1970 Chevrolet and undertook the long journey to their new home. Martín had attended school in California for only a few months because, after he was beaten up by kids in a gang, he and his mother agreed that it would be dangerous for him to go to school. He was too small to defend himself, and he could not speak enough English to seek the help of others at school.

I met Martín in April 1995, in Iowa, as a 13-year-old seventh grader. In the mornings he attended Central Campus, where the Sioux City Community School District Reception Center is located, and in the afternoons he attended Woodrow Wilson Middle School. Martín seemed to have adjusted well to life in Sioux City, enjoying the calmness and friendliness of the place. He liked school but read and wrote slowly and with difficulty. He tried hard to catch up and received much support from his teachers, but he was concerned that yet another family move could disrupt his studies and his newly found sense of security.

• **Igor** grew up in Russia, where he attended school regularly, was an excellent student, and enjoyed his childhood and early adolescence. In 1993, when he was 14, his family moved to New York. Igor had studied some English in school, but like the rest of his family, he knew only a few phrases. His father had been an elementary school teacher in Russia, but in New York, with extremely limited English skills, he could only get a job as a janitor in a department store. Igor's father studied English at night and dreamed of some day working in a school again. Igor and his family lived in Astoria, Queens, where they kept in close contact with the Russian community. At first, Igor attended a neighborhood high school, but in 1994, encouraged by immigrant friends of the family, he transferred to International High School, where he was a 17-year-old junior when I met him.

At home, the family conversed in Russian, and Igor, his two younger brothers, and his teenage friends spoke Russian with the adults in their circle. Among themselves, they spoke English.

A warm, open, and energetic young man, Igor had made friends easily. At school he spoke primarily English, except when he talked with other Russian-speaking students who were new to the school. His English had developed rapidly since his arrival, and he could read fairly well in English. He still did not understand everything in his school texts but knew how to persevere and be patient. When he wrote in English he made errors, but, as he put it, he felt he had "come a long way." Though he was not sure about his future career plans, there was little doubt that through hard work, Igor would be able to achieve what he set out to do.

• **Huung Suu** is a slim, serious student from Vietnam. After having been separated from their parents for 5 years, he and his older brother were able to join them in Iowa in 1994. Huung Suu had gone to school in Vietnam until seventh grade, then learned to be a tailor, sewing in a small shop with his brother to support himself. When I met him, he was a 19-year-old ninth grader in Sioux City, Iowa, where in the mornings he attended North High and in the afternoons went to the Sioux City Community School District Reception Center to study English and receive tutoring in Vietnamese. When Huung Suu first arrived, he knew only a few words in English. A year later, he could participate in conversations in English and was making progress in school.

At home, Huung Suu spoke to his parents and brother in Vietnamese, and in the high school, he spoke primarily English. He told me that speaking English was very tiring because he must be attentive to every minute detail to make sense of what was going on. He usually missed much of what was discussed in his classes but had noticed that he was beginning to improve. In the afternoons, he attended an English as a second language (ESL) class and was tutored by a Vietnamese-speaking aide on his morning subjects. He worked diligently to catch up, and the welcoming atmosphere of the Reception Center helped relieve the tensions of the morning. In the evenings, while his father worked in a Chinese-Vietnamese restaurant, his mother embroidered, and his brother worked at a tailoring job, Huung Suu sat at the kitchen table, grappling with new concepts and ways of expressing ideas.

• **Monique** is a vivacious 15-year-old Haitian student at Edison High School in Dade County, Florida. For 8 years in Haiti, since her mother died, she had taken on the full responsibility of two younger siblings; cooking, cleaning, running the house, and bargaining for deals at the marketplace in her village, which left her no time to attend school.

In 1994 her father, who had been saving money for the trip for years, in spite of economic hardships, suddenly asked Monique to pack two pieces of clothing for each child and food for a sea journey to Miami. The decision was so sudden that Monique did not have time to say good-bye to her neighbor, a kind woman who had taught her how to care for her family. This she remembers with sadness. A few weeks after their arrival in the United States, she discovered through "the Haitian network" that the high school had a special program for students who had never been to school before, and Monique started attending school for the first time in her life. Her siblings attended an extended-day-care program provided by the county while she went to school, and her father looked for odd jobs during the day. None of the family had immigration papers.

Monique told me she would like to become a teacher one day, for she knows the power that teachers have to open possibilities for all children, especially for those like herself who need so much support to succeed. Her teacher kept telling her that her dream was possible. Her father also encouraged her, and she worked diligently in school. She was making progress, but there was still so much to catch up with. Every time she moved one step, everybody else in her regular classes seemed to have moved two or three. Despite her enthusiasm, hard work, and determination, and despite the kindness and support of the school and the New Beginnings program (a newcomer program for underschooled students), she sometimes wondered whether catching up was possible at all.

In her neighborhood and at home, Monique usually spoke Haitian Creole. She avoided interacting with many of the neighborhood teenagers because some seemed rough, and they laughed at her because she took studying seriously. In school she and her friends, other ESL students in the New Beginnings program, practiced English with each other.

• **Carlos**'s parents moved to the Salinas Valley in California from Pátzcuaro, Mexico, in 1982, 3 years before he was born. In 1988, hoping that he would learn English more effectively if they placed him in a school with no programs in Spanish, the Medinas moved to the southern part of Salinas, where most of the city's English-speaking population lives. Carlos did acceptably well in school until he reached the third grade, when everything became extremely difficult for him. He could not understand what was going on in class, became a discipline problem, and was suspended from school. His worried parents transferred him to an all-Spanish program in another district. This did not help. Unable to understand the teacher's explanations in Spanish, Carlos received low grades and was barely promoted to fourth grade. In middle school in yet another school district, Carlos was still classified as Limited English Proficient, attended classes in English as a second language, and took his subject matter classes in Spanish, which he found extremely difficult.

When I met Carlos in 1995, he was a freshman in high school. He was uninterested in school, often cutting classes and considering dropping out. He had a sense, developed through many years of discontinuity, confusion, and failure, that he would never be able to catch up. Carlos read poorly in English and Spanish, and although he could talk to his friends in either language quite comfortably, this ability did not carry him through his classes. In class he had to make a tremendous effort to understand what the teacher was saying, and if he was called upon, he felt that "se me hacen bolas," everything became tied up, and he could not express himself. The fear that he might be called upon in class interfered with his ability to pay attention to what was being said. As a consequence, he was increasingly drawn to other teenagers who, like himself, were disengaged from school.

Carlos's father had seasonal work in the lettuce and strawberry fields. Fortunately, he was able to take advantage of the Amnesty program and get his and his wife's immigration papers in order in 1993. His two children, having been born in the United States, did not have any legal problems. Carlos's mother cleaned houses, making as much money as her husband in half of the time he spent laboring in the fields. She was concerned when Carlos skipped school but did not know how to help him. She was never able to attend school, and even visiting a school was not easy for her. The one time she went to the high school to find out about her son's low grades, she had to wait for a long time before being told that she did not need to worry, that his grades were not too bad.

At home and in the neighborhood, the family spoke Spanish. Carlos and his friends spoke both English and Spanish, depending on the situation, but mostly they "just fool around in English." Carlos tried to convey the appearance of somebody who did not care about school or his future, but I sensed that underneath his bravado, he wished for a more promising future.

• **Marisela**, 15 years old, is the daughter of a Brazilian architect who, after practicing his profession in Brazil successfully for 20 years, received a job offer in Miami and decided to move to the United States with his family. In Rio de Janeiro, Marisela had attended a private bilingual school, where she studied in French and Portuguese. She had just started learning English as a subject in school when the family left Brazil. In elementary school Marisela and her classmates had learned some English, and outside of school they kept up with the lyrics of American songs.

When I met her, Marisela attended Miami Beach High, where she was enrolled as a ninth grader in 2 periods of ESL classes and subject-matter courses in Spanish. Marisela had never studied Spanish formally, but like most Brazilians, she could understand Spanish because of its similarity to Portuguese. Being already bilingual, the acquisition of third and fourth languages came easily to her. She was delighted that she could improve her Spanish (which for the time being made the serious coursework easy) while learning English.

Marisela, dedicated and hardworking, pretty and self-assured, was not only a good student, she was also one of the most popular girls in school. She thrived on socializing and being able to practice her English and Spanish. She was doing so well in English that during the second semester, with the approval of her counselor, she changed to mainstream math and science classes, conducted solely in English.

She spoke Portuguese with her family, although both of her parents spoke English well. She had a few Brazilian friends with whom she also interacted in Portuguese, but other than that, the rest of her day was spent speaking both English and Spanish. Her plans for the future were to become an interpreter because "you get to travel all the time, and you meet all kinds of interesting and diverse people."

Factors That Shape Immigrant Students' Needs and School Success

In all their diversity, the students profiled above represent, in different configurations, the key factors shaping the educational needs of immigrant students in secondary schools in the United States. Their shared situations include learning English as a second language and migrating with their families to this country. They differ in other key ways, including such factors as their language ability (in both English and their native language), their parents' English language skills and educational profiles, their academic backgrounds, their immigration status (legal or illegal), their economic status and success both in their home countries and in the United States, the amount of trauma they experienced in their home country and during the move to the United States, their families' expectations and support, and their stability in the American educational system. Society's perceptions of them as legal or illegal immigrants—especially in the wake of strong anti-immigrant feelings and legal efforts to restrict immigrants' schooling in California[1]—or as refugees also affect their schooling and the development of their cultural identities. In various ways, these factors can enhance or inhibit the ability of immigrant students to succeed in American schools and to achieve their dreams.

Four of the students described in the profiles fit the standard definition of immigrants who are in the process of learning English as a second language. Students like Monique, with little previous schooling and practically no literacy in her native language, and Carlos, with little academic proficiency in any language, constitute special cases. Carlos, being U.S.-born, is not an immigrant. Yet there are many teenagers like him—long-term ESL students who have developed a conversational

---

1. Proposition 187, passed by the California electorate in 1994 and subsequently challenged in the courts and under arbitration, eliminates public education and health services to undocumented immigrants. In 1998, California voters passed Proposition 227, "English for the children," which eliminates bilingual schooling—schooling in two languages—unless parents request and sign a cumbersome petition that their children receive these services. It limits the teaching of English as second language to one year.

competence in their family language and in English, but who neverthe-less do not appear to have sufficient linguistic competence in either language to succeed in the increasingly sophisticated course work demanded in secondary schools. These students' language proficiencies pose unique challenges to their schooling, but because they do not fit the standard definition of *immigrant* (born outside the United States), they have not received adequate attention. I include Carlos in my discussion because more attention to the predicament of students like him is needed (see Suárez-Orozco, 1989, for discussion).

Socioeconomic Status and Previous Academic Achievement

Students' socioeconomic status and previous academic achievement can strongly affect their educational experiences in U.S. schools. Some students come from affluent middle class families, their parents entering the United States with professional strengths and privileges made possible by their education. The students, coming to the United States also with previous rigorous educations, build on their strengths in this country, which affects how well they do in school in general (Gibson, 1993). Marisela, for example, thought that she would be able to move out of the English as a second language program by the following year, after having attended for 2 years. By then, she expected to be able to understand and use enough English to succeed in regular classes taught exclusively in English. In fact, the Brazilian school she had attended (an exclusive private school) was far more rigorous than what she encountered in the United States. "I know that academically I will be able to do very well because I have always been a good student, and after this summer I should know enough English to be in the regular classes," she told me confidently. Marisela's parents were both professionals, working in their fields and doing well financially. They expected Marisela and her brother to go to the university and to get good jobs.

Other students, such as Igor, also come with rigorous academic educations, but their well-educated parents lack the language and contacts in the United States to obtain professional level jobs in this country. As is typical of many immigrants in similar situations, his parents were willing to take menial jobs and study hard themselves in order to secure a better future for their children (Suárez-Orozco, 1996; Tuan, 1995). Igor's father told me, "I don't care how many jobs I have to work to support the family here. It is too late for me to make true the dream to be a teacher in this country. . . . We came to this country thinking of the future of our children. They will live the dream for us." Igor and his father share a dream that is made possible through education; they will discover together how to achieve it.

Other students come to the United States with some schooling, although interrupted, and have more modest socioeconomic backgrounds. Often their parents did not complete basic schooling in their home countries, and they are not professionals. For these students, who lack Marisela's social and academic background, academic progress and development of English skills is slower and more painful. Huung Suu is one of them. In many states he would not be eligible for a regular high school education because of his age (he was 19 years old in the ninth grade), but in Iowa students can attend high school until the age of 21. In fact, 22-year-old students who are close to graduation and desire to stay in school until graduation are allowed to do so (D. Chávez, Iowa State Department of Education, personal communication, April 1995).

Other students, like Monique, arrive in the United States with practically no previous schooling because of economically precarious or violent conditions in their home countries. These students need a great deal of support from their schools and families, and it takes them longer to develop literacy skills in English. Monique was learning to read and write for the first time at the age of 15. Fortunately, she had excellent teachers in the New Beginnings program at Edison High School in Dade County, Florida. Because of her age, she had been classified as a freshman, but she was not ready to handle the mainstream subject matter courses the way they were regularly taught at the school. She needed the support of the New Beginnings program beyond the 2 years it was designed to serve students. She also needed the support

of mainstream teachers who could expand their instructional repertoire to make the curriculum accessible to English learners. It is difficult to predict what will become of Monique.

Immigration Status

Another important aspect of immigrant students' backgrounds is their
immigration status, which can affect both their sense of security and
their cultural identity. Marisela's family migrated to the United States
legally, and both her parents had H-1 visas, which are offered to foreign
professionals whose expertise is needed in this country. They knew
they would maintain their connections to Brazil and the friends they
left there through regular visits. Learning English and studying in an
American high school did not threaten their children's Brazilian identity and language; it simply enriched their individual experience.

Being a legal immigrant to the United States may confer a sense of security, but it does not guarantee acceptance by others in the country.
How members of the wider society, both inside and outside of school,
view immigrants and refugees also shapes students' educational experiences. Huung Suu, for example, was in the United States legally, which
made it possible for him to study and work in his new environment
without fear. He knew, though, that he was not welcomed by everybody in the community. Although acknowledging this made him sad,
it also strengthened his resolve to study and work hard.

Being here illegally exacerbates the problems of students like Monique.
Monique did not feel welcome at Edison High School outside of the
New Beginnings classes. With a new wave of sentiment against illegal
immigrants in this country, the situation for her and others can only
worsen. Other students, like Igor, have refugee status, which can be
perceived negatively or positively, depending on the political and social
mood. In any case, the students' immigration status can deeply affect
their motivation, confidence, and sense of cultural identity, all of which
shape their educational experiences. An elementary school teacher's
documentary film, *P.O.V.: Fear and Learning at Hoover Elementary*

(Simon, 1997)—winner of the Freedom of Expession award at the Sundance Film Festival in Ogden, Utah—clearly shows the negative impact of Proposition 187, which encouraged some teachers and library staff in a school to oppose openly the presence of their immigrant students.

Family Support and Expectations

The support and expectations of immigrant students' families are crucial to their education, though high expectations can also create intense pressure to succeed. Huung Suu's brother and parents wanted him to go to a university and study to be a professional. He studied diligently in order to live up to the family's dream, knowing that other young men in the community had been able to do it and feeling that he would be able to do it, too. He proudly showed me a present his brother had given him, a mini computer that translates between English and Vietnamese and pronounces the English words. One of his teachers explained that these translating machines are quite expensive for a family that can barely make ends meet, but that the gift symbolizes the expectations the family had for Huung Suu. They hoped he would graduate from high school, attend a community college, and transfer to a university. Because Huung Suu had a trade at which he was well skilled, it was possible for him to make a living in Sioux City as he had done in Vietnam, even if he did not pursue postsecondary education. Both he and his family wanted him to continue studying after high school graduation.

Parental support can be "interventionist" or "noninterventionist" vis-à-vis the school (Bhachu, 1985, quoted in Gibson, 1995, p. 86). Sometimes schools tend to interpret direct intervention, as manifested by school visits, attendance at meetings, participation in school-site councils, and so on, as the sole indicator of parental support for the academic endeavors of their children. However, as has been demonstrated by Bhachu through studies of Punjabi Sikh students in Great Britain and by Gibson (1993) focusing on Punjabi Sikh students in California, families that rarely or never visit the school, meet with teachers, or participate in school events may also be supporting their children's schooling by creating a home atmosphere that communicates the importance of success through studies.

Language Proficiencies

Immigrant students' language proficiencies have a tremendous impact on their ability to succeed in American schools. But we often overlook the language problems of students like Carlos, a second-generation immigrant who struggled with both English and Spanish. These students' language abilities suffer because in the current political climate, students are pushed from one language to another too rapidly to allow them to develop communicative competence in either one. Teenagers like Carlos fall victim to society's desire for a rapid transition to English, but they are unable to do academic work either in their mother tongue or in English. For these students, neither the linguistic norms of the mother tongue nor those of the target language, English, are available as resources for the kinds of tasks that school demands, and they find it difficult to participate in classes of either language. Although it could be said that Carlos spoke both English and Spanish, it could also be said that he knew neither.

Educational Continuity in the United States

Many immigrant families move often from one school to another within a school district or from district to district. The resulting lack of academic continuity can cause major difficulties for students trying to adjust to a new culture, learn a new language, and master academic content. It is not uncommon to find immigrant students in secondary schools who have traveled through native language instruction, English-only instruction, and different types of bilingual education several times in a few years (Minicucci & Olsen, 1992). While a district may have a general policy for the education of students learning English (who are often termed LEP, Limited English Proficient), this policy is usually cast in vague and imprecise terms. In most cases, individual schools are in charge of developing their own ways of educating their English language learners, which sometimes results in two or three fundamentally different approaches to educating these students within the same school district. Well-thought-out, coherent educational plans are the exception in the education of English language learners at the secondary school level (Minicucci & Olsen, 1992; Multicultural Education, Training, and Advocacy, Inc. [META], 1995).

Social Challenges and Sense of Self

Immigrant and U.S.-born English language learners contend with many difficult challenges, which are not purely linguistic. As Luis Rodríguez (1993) describes in his own story, English learners also struggle with the intolerance of the majority population at the same time that they are seeking a sense of identity, self-expression, and self-worth.

I had fallen through the chasm between two languages. The Spanish had been beaten out of me in the early years of school—and I didn't learn English very well either.

This was the predicament of many Chicanos.

We could almost be called incommunicable. . . .

Our expressive powers were strong and vibrant. If these could be nurtured, if language skills could be developed, we could break through any communication barrier. We needed to obtain victories in language built on an infrastructure of self-worth.

But we were often defeated from the start. (p. 219)

The story of Luis Rodríguez is similar to that of many immigrant teenagers who attend mainstream schools. They enter school as members of a marginalized population, and their marginalization is reinforced by the operating structures of the institution (Spindler & Spindler, 1993), often unintentionally. With minority[2] second language learners, schools often focus solely on their acquisition of English while ignoring their social integration, sense of self, and academic progress. This

---

2. *Minority* is the label commonly assigned to groups on the basis of their gender, ethnicity, race, religion, or social class. In conceptualizations of *minority*, numbers matter less than power; thus, the term is applied to groups with comparatively less power and fewer rights and privileges than more dominant groups (Tollefson, 1994).

focus can limit their opportunities for succeeding socially and economically in the future.

Practices That Address Immigrant Students' Needs

A number of practices have been suggested to address the factors described above. They include the explicit teaching of the rules of the *culture of power* (Delpit, 1995) to minority students. The rules guiding academic work in schools, for example, are norms that have been appropriated by successful majority students through a process of socialization that has taken place gradually over a long period of time. For newcomers, these rules are not evident, and it is almost impossible to discern that they are in operation. In many cultures, for example, it is perfectly appropriate that two or more people speak at the same time. In American English, and especially in American classrooms, the norm is that one person speaks at a time. Students new to the American school system who do not know the rule will violate it, and they will not understand why people resent their behavior. Rules for appropriate participation in classes, then, need to be explicitly taught, so that they can be understood and complied with when necessary.

Engaging both majority and minority students in a process of *cultural therapy* (Spindler & Spindler, 1993) is another approach in which features of one's own culture and those of other cultures are brought to conscious awareness. Potential conflicts and misunderstandings between cultures are discussed as arising from cultural features that can be interesting to study objectively, without becoming emotionally involved. In the authors' words, cultural therapy makes it possible to discuss these features as a "third presence, removed somewhat from the person, so that one's actions can be taken as caused by one's culture and not by one's personality" (p. 28).

A third approach is exemplified by the European Language Project (Twitching, 1993), in which teachers work in guided groups to analyze videotapes of their teaching of minority students, identify problem areas, and discuss possible solutions among themselves.

These three practices acknowledge that the combined challenges of educating minority students and of directly addressing cultural differences and social inequalities involve everyone—students, teachers, administrators and other school personnel, and society at large. These approaches defy the prevailing perception that it is the responsibility of immigrant students to adapt to and tolerate the status quo. In a poignant example from her work in the Central Valley in California, Margaret Gibson reports that Punjabi newcomers and even second generation Punjabi students were asked by a teacher to tolerate verbal and even physical abuse triggered by their White classmates' prejudice and ignorance (Gibson, 1993). The future success of a multicultural society can only be predicated on everybody's efforts to adapt to and interact with each other and on schools structured as "moving mosaics" (Hargreaves, 1994, p. 62) with flexible structures that enable all members of the school community to respond effectively to the ever-changing needs of a complex society.

Whatever the approach, in the education of immigrant students (as in the education of all children) it is necessary to recognize and build on the identity, language, and knowledge that they already possess. Educators must provide students with avenues to explore and strengthen their ethnic identities and languages while developing their ability to engage in the valued discourses of this country. One identity and language does not need to develop at the expense of another. Many cases of successful immigrant students show that conscious accommodation without assimilation into the mainstream society is possible (see, for example, Gibson, 1995).

To reinforce this point, I turn to the Spindlers' (1993) notions of the *enduring, situated,* and *endangered* self. The enduring self has a sense of continuity with its own past, a continuity of experience, meaning, and social identity. The situated self is contextualized and instrumental and changes selectively to meet the demands of everyday life. When the enduring self is violated too often and too strongly by the demands of the situated self, it is damaged and becomes the endangered self. For immigrant students, the enduring self is what they bring with them from their previous lives in other countries; after arrival, their situated self adapts to handle the demands of living in a new culture. The enduring self needs to be reinforced, and the situated self needs to be developed for immigrant students to succeed.

This is what many minority students with strong ethnic identities must do. They must keep their identity, since this identity, in the sense of the enduring self, is essential to the maintenance of life itself. And yet they must get along in the world as it is. It is a world where instrumental competencies have to be acquired that are not required by the enduring self or one's own ethnic identity; a sense of pervasive self-efficacy must be developed in order to cope with the exigencies of life as they happen in a complex technological society. (Spindler & Spindler, 1993, p. 41)

Luis Rodríguez (1993), quoted above, was fortunate because he found a caring teacher who helped him to expand his knowledge about Mexican culture and history, which gave him pride and comfort in his identity. He was also supported in meeting the challenge of adapting to new situations, and he gained the critical perspective to maintain balance between his identity and these situations. Rodríguez's personal story points to the importance of mentors in the lives of immigrant teenagers. Ms. Baez, a Chicana teacher, inspired the troubled young Luis and his peers and helped them to complete high school. Luis Rodríguez became an artist and an accomplished writer who has dedicated his life to providing marginalized, powerless youngsters with the tools to make their own adaptations. He conducts writing workshops for students who are at risk of failing school and for youth in juvenile halls. He often speaks to educators and policy makers about the need to reconsider how we currently work with minority students.

Rodríguez was fortunate. When the enduring self (the self of the past and the home culture and language) is not recognized and valued, the endangered self can prevail, with drastic, destructive educational and personal consequences. In "Nobody Could See I Was a Finn" (in

Skutnabb-Kangas, 1981, pp. 318-321), an autobiographical piece that transports us to the traumatic experiences of attending school in Sweden, Antti Jalava provides a powerful example of what so many immigrants feel. Even after having completed high school, he felt worthless and suicidal because his Finnish self had been destroyed, and yet he knew that neither the diploma he held nor the Swedish he spoke would amount to much because he had learned "street" Swedish and his high school work had consisted of low-level courses. He was condemned to a future of low expectations. His once-blossoming Finnish had atrophied; he could not even scream his agony in his once-beloved native language.

The effective education of immigrant students requires sensitivity to all aspects of their former and current lives. While we must always see our students as the unique individuals they are, we also need to create programs that take their shared attributes into account without assuming that they are all the same. The factors discussed above—their previous schooling, English and native language abilities, family and community support systems, immigration status, and economic and social status in the United States—are some of the essential attributes we need to consider as we seek to understand the immigrant students in our schools and programs.

Second Language Learning and the Schooling of Immigrant Adolescents

Understanding the variety of backgrounds that immigrant students of secondary school age bring to their schooling in the United States is critical to educating them well. We also need to understand the complex processes of second language acquisition that research and theory have elucidated to date. In addition, we need to understand the larger social and cultural issues that shape the education of immigrant students, such as prejudice, social alienation, and gang activities.

Some Common Misconceptions

Misconceptions about second language learning affect educators' and the general public's perceptions of English learners and the establishment of policies and practices regarding language education in schools. The following discussion focuses on some of the most damaging misconceptions affecting the education of immigrant students at the secondary school level (see McLaughlin, 1992).

Misconception 1—Learning English as quickly as possible is the first priority for immigrant students.

For a long time, the effective teaching of English has been considered the major task of educators working with immigrant teenagers in American schools. In the minds of many, English should be taught and learned as quickly as possible (Chávez, 1995; Peterson, 1993). However, although language development is part of the purpose of any schooling (Bernstein, 1972; Heath, 1983)—whether it takes place in the family language or in a second language—its focus and form change as the curriculum develops from grade to grade. In the lower elementary grades—from kindergarten to second grade—students primarily learn to read and write and are socialized into the culture of the school. Beginning in third grade, students increasingly read and write in order to learn. At the upper elementary and secondary school levels, cognitive and academic development are central to the notion of schooling, and the role of language development shifts to support these other aspects of learning.

Successfully teaching immigrant adolescents to speak English alone is not sufficient to enable them to succeed in American middle and high schools, where they will be required to perform at sophisticated cognitive levels in subject-specific areas. If a narrow focus is placed on immigrant students' development of English, how will they ever catch up academically with their native English-speaking counterparts? As Collier (1995) points out, native English-speaking students do not wait until their English is fully developed before achieving at high academic levels; they are continuously expanding their linguistic and cognitive abilities in English. At the same time, the success of English learners, paradoxically, depends on much more than learning English. It also involves facility with the central concepts, canons, and discourses associated with different disciplines.

Misconception 2—If students can converse in English, they can succeed in mainstream courses taught in English.

It is sometimes assumed in schools that students' ability to participate in everyday oral communication is a valid measure of their competence to use language in a wide variety of settings, including demanding academic work. However, social and academic uses of language are very different (see Cazden, 1988; Heath, 1983). The differences between school demands and social experiences can make it difficult for English language learners to work with academic content, unless a great deal of instructional and linguistic support is provided (Delpit, 1995; Lambert & Cazabon, 1994; Tharp & Gallimore, 1988).

On the basis of this misconception, immigrant students are promoted from ESL classes into mainstream classes (conducted exclusively in English) on the basis of their conversational ability alone and are given no academic or linguistic support. As a result, they often lag behind their native English-speaking counterparts in academic progress. As Cummins (1979) argued, there may be two dimensions of communicative competence, which he called Basic Interpersonal Communicative Skills (BICS) and Cognitive Academic Language Proficiency

(CALP). BICS referred to the ability to use a language in face-to-face situations, when the repair of breakdowns in communication is easily negotiable. CALP referred to the ability to use the language in situations in which the content is decontextualized and cognitively demanding, such as the ability needed by a 10th grader in California to read and discuss a text on the socioeconomic conditions prevalent in prerevolutionary France.

Second language learners may fail academically because their promotion into English-only classes is made on an assessment of their BICS and not of their CALP. Cummins (1981) has since elaborated the BICS/CALP dichotomy into two intersecting continua with a range of cognitive demands and contextual support involved in specific language activities, but the key distinction between conversational and academic linguistic proficiency remains important.

Another factor to be considered when moving English language learners into regular academic classes taught in English is the subject matter being taught. The rule of thumb used to be to place students first in math and science courses, and then in social studies and literature courses. This principle was based on the belief that the linguistic demands of social studies and literature courses are greater than those of solving mathematical problems and conducting laboratory experiments. However, math and science courses require students not only to solve number problems and use mathematical formulas, but also to evaluate, compare, contrast, hypothesize, and elaborate conclusions using both oral and written language (Cohen, McLaughlin, & Talbert, 1993). Satisfactory performance in these subjects requires the use of complex and sophisticated subject-specific discourse. Even in elementary school science, children develop compelling arguments and interpretations of observed phenomena. In order to perform these tasks in English, they need a sophisticated knowledge of the language.

Misconception 3—Native languages are a crutch that impedes students' progress in English.

Opponents of native language instruction often argue that the time taken to teach in the native language reduces the time available for exposure to English, thus reducing the rate of English learning. They assume that more exposure to English is better. A related assumption is that the first language interferes with the second language, so that the chances for second language proficiency are increased if the first language is excluded from instruction as much as possible. The Direct Method, for example, is based on discouraging or prohibiting teachers and students from using the native language of learners in class (see Doggett, 1994). A third assumption is that students will not learn the second language if the first language is available for communication and academic instruction. In such situations, proponents of this belief argue, students are not motivated to learn the second language because they do not need it to communicate.

This triple argument of *exposure, interference,* and *need* is a powerful force against the use of students' native languages in school, sometimes even in the home. What arguments could possibly be posed in favor of continued first-language use? Exposure to the second language is clearly important; however, the quality of the exposure is more important than its quantity. Just as time on task does not in itself produce learning, extensive exposure to English does not in itself promote the learning of English. Key to the learning of a language are access and engagement—understanding or participating in second language events and being attentive and emotionally involved with learning the language.

Cummins's (1981) interdependence hypothesis refutes the notion that maximum exposure to the second language as soon as possible enhances the speed of acquisition of the language and the academic performance of its learners. After reviewing several studies, Cummins concludes that the development of students' first language cognitive and academic skills is as important as exposure to the second language for the development of cognitive-academic skills in the second language.

The interdependence hypothesis helps explain in part why Igor and Marisela were making such gains with their English language learning. They studied in their first language for a considerable amount of time, which created a cognitive base from which they could draw as they developed a second language. This hypothesis also throws light on Carlos's and Monique's difficulties. They had no academic facility in their native languages. As will be seen later, coursework conducted in Haitian Creole was not only beneficial, but became a cornerstone in Monique's eventual academic success.

Misconception 4—All adolescent immigrants will progress at the same rate in learning English.

It is common knowledge that students with different personal circumstances perform differently on academic tasks at their grade level. Thus, it seems natural to assume that students will vary considerably in the amount of time it takes to learn academic English. In a 10-year longitudinal study, Virginia Collier and Wayne Thomas from George Mason University (Collier, 1995) analyzed data from five school districts, a sample of approximately 42,000 language minority school children per year, to answer a frequently asked question: How long does it take immigrant students to learn English well enough to perform successfully in academic mainstream classes? The answer is that it varies a great deal. It may take students who are learning English anywhere from 4 to 10 years to reach the 50th Normal Curve Equivalent (NCE) or percentile on standardized tests in English, depending on their personal histories and the educational context.

Language acquisition, both first and subsequent, at whatever age, is an arduous task requiring enormous investments of time, attention, effort, and emotional engagement. Some researchers (McLaughlin, 1992, for example) argue that teenagers are intrinsically better language learners than either younger or older learners, since a teenager already has a well developed cognitive base and learning skills. On the other hand, the linguistic and conceptual sophistication required of teenagers is greater than that required of young children. While children may need only to be surrounded by a language in a positive climate and at a level they can comprehend (Krashen, 1985) to acquire it, teenagers need much more than exposure to comprehensible language. They must be involved and engaged in communicative events in order to profit from them and develop communicative competence. The length of time it will take individual students to develop this competence cannot be predicted accurately. This is especially true for immigrant teenagers who have so much to learn about academic English. Even given optimal learning environments in American schools, teenagers require varying amounts of time to learn English, according to their prior levels of schooling, academic achievement, and development of their primary language.

Misconception 5—Immigrant students' academic progress depends solely on individual motivation.

Immigrant students may seem to their teachers to be withdrawn. This withdrawal is often misconstrued as a lack of motivation, when it may stem more from their fear of failure and from a sense that teachers do not truly expect them to succeed. Instead of blaming the students for their lack of motivation, teachers need to ask themselves the following questions: What kinds of norms, values, beliefs, and expectations are being conveyed through spoken and unspoken messages delivered in class every day? How are immigrant students made to feel about their capabilities and possibilities for success? Does the climate of the class make students feel capable, valued, challenged, and supported? Are they continuously being provided with opportunities for development of their conceptual, academic, and linguistic capabilities?

When immigrant students experience a mismatch between the worlds of their family, their peers, and their school, they will withdraw, and success will be sporadic. In classrooms where immigrant students do well, "teachers know the students well, are attuned to their needs, and show personal concerns for their lives. These teachers are aware of their students' precarious academic status and incorporate various peda-gogical methods to ensure student involvement" (Phelan, Davidson, & Cao, 1991, p. 245). Involvement is possible because students are mo-tivated by the assurance that teachers think they are capable, value the knowledge they bring to the classroom, and will help them achieve beyond their current level of competence (Abi-Nader, 1993; Lucas, Henze, & Donato, 1990; Moll & Diaz, 1993).

Closely tied to the misconception that English language learners them-selves are solely responsible for how much English they learn and how rapidly they learn it are the myths that American schools (1) provide the same opportunities for all students and (2) function in rational ways. Many people think of schools as great social equalizers that care-fully plan success for all students, but most English language learners come from economically disadvantaged backgrounds and attend schools with high concentrations of poverty (August & Hakuta, 1997). These schools do not provide coherent programs for their students, but rather respond to educational challenges reactive, piecemeal ap-proaches that do not help immigrants—or other students—to achieve. English language learners therefore face not only the challenge of learn-ing a second language, but also the challenge of attending schools ill prepared to educate them.

The misconceptions discussed above misrepresent the needs of immi-grant students and present overly simplistic approaches to second lan-guage learning. The reality of immigrant students' needs is much more complex, as the six student profiles in chapter 1 show. Instead of bas-ing our instructional programs on these misconceptions, we need to be guided by a solid understanding of the nature of second language acquisition informed by current research and theory.

The Complex Processes of Second Language Acquisition

More important than discussions about the advantages of one teaching method or another is understanding contextual factors and how they may affect students' learning opportunities. We must assume that all students are intrinsically capable of adequate language development and able to do well in school, but that a host of factors may enhance or impede their language development and academic progress.

We can examine these contextual factors by considering second language learning from several different perspectives, which include the language, the learner, and the learning process. Each of these perspectives has its individual, social, and societal aspects, as visually represented in Table 1, which shows some of the many factors that influence the second language learning process. The complexity illustrated here discourages simplistic views of language learning. We must realize that learning—especially language learning—is not always the result of teaching, and that teaching does not necessarily lead to learning. We need to understand the complexity of language learning from a variety of perspectives. Learning a language, which is central to our thoughts and social relationships, cannot be reduced to a simple transmission of facts and automated skills.

Language

A number of factors related to students' first and second languages shape their language learning, including the linguistic distance between the two languages; the level of proficiency in the native language and prior knowledge of the second language; whether the native language is a nonstandard or standard dialect; the status of the languages; and sociolinguistic attitudes toward them.

Table 1. Perspectives on Second Language Learning

	Individual	**Social**	**Societal**
Language	Native language (distance, proficiency) Second language knowledge	Dialect vs. standard Language attitudes	Status of L1/L2
Learner	Needs and goals	Peer groups Home support Role models	Integrative/instrumental orientation Acceptance Opportunities
Learning	Learning styles	Motivation Classroom interaction	Expectations Support

Language distance

Second language development is first of all influenced by the linguistic distance between the native language and the target language. That is, languages can be comparatively more or less difficult to learn, depending on how different from or similar they are to the languages the learner already knows. At the Defense Language Institute in Monterey, California, for example, languages are placed in four different categories, depending on their average learning difficulty (from the perspective of the native English speaker). The basic intensive language course, which brings a student to an intermediate level, can be as short as 24 weeks for languages such as Dutch or Spanish, or as long as 65 weeks for languages such as Arabic, Korean, or Vietnamese.

Native language proficiency

Another factor that needs to be taken into account is the level of proficiency the student has reached in the native language. This refers not only to attainment in oral language and literacy, but also to metalinguistic development, training in formal and academic features of language use, knowledge of rhetorical patterns and variations in genre and style, and so on. The more academically sophisticated the student's native language knowledge and abilities are, the easier it will be for that student to add a second language to his or her repertoire. This observation may help explain why foreign exchange students tend to be successful in American high school classes: They already have high school level proficiency in their native language.

Knowledge of the second language

In addition to varying levels of native language development, high school students have varying amounts of prior knowledge of English, ranging from conversational skills acquired from contacts with the English-speaking world, to formal (mostly grammatical) knowledge obtained in English as a foreign language classes in their countries of origin. An effective program needs to use the students' prior knowledge as a basis for further development, while at the same time being aware of the specific demands that a student's language history may place on second language learning. For example, a student with informal conversational English skills, picked up in the street or around the neighborhood, may have little understanding of English grammatical systems. Such a learner may face severe difficulties in developing grammatical competence, since this involves a regression from a comfortable though superficial conversational fluency, almost going back to a communicative "square one" in order to eventually achieve a more grammatically elaborated linguistic proficiency. This is, psychologically as well as linguistically, a difficult and protracted process (see Higgs & Clifford, 1982).

Dialect and register

At the social level, learners may need to learn a dialect and register in school that differ from the ones they are used to hearing in their daily lives. It is natural to resist, consciously or unconsciously, acquiring speech patterns that differ significantly from more familiar ones. Such patterns seem unnatural or even a betrayal of one's loyalties to a particular group or philosophy.

Language attitudes

Language attitudes in the learner, the peer group, the school, the neighborhood, and society at large can have an enormous effect on the second language learning process, both positive and negative. It is vital that teachers and students themselves examine and understand these attitudes and realize that second language acquisition is the *addition* of new repertoires, not the *replacement* of one's known and trusted variety with another, possibly alien one.

This is true not only in the teaching of English as a second language, but even in the teaching of subject matter in students' native languages, whenever that is a possibility in school. I have been told by students in Spanish for Native Speakers classes in California (which follow the English Language Arts curriculum through literary texts originally written in Spanish, or translated into Spanish) that they feel bad when teachers tell them that the way they speak Spanish is not right, that people do not speak that way ("No se dice así"). "That's the way everybody I know speaks. Why is she saying nobody speaks that way?" they respond. Clearly, this is an issue of dialectal or register difference. School requires formal registers and standard dialects, while conversation with friends and relatives calls for informal registers and oftentimes nonstandard dialects. If, in order to speak the "schooled" way, students have to deny the way their loved ones interact, they may not be willing to learn or use the new variety. If, instead, their expressive ways are valued when used in appropriate contexts, new discourses will not replace them. Rather, the new discourses will expand students' communicative repertoires and promote academic success.

Addressing the issues of dialect, register, and language attitudes calls for enhancing teachers' knowledge about language varieties during preservice and inservice education.

Language status

Consideration of dialects and registers and the relationship between two languages also involves the relative prestige of different languages and their related cultural and ethnic associations. If a student's first language has a very low status vis á vis the second, then second language acquisition can be more difficult and problematic, since it involves overcoming a psychological as well as a social gap. In addition, learners who manage to make this jump may lose their native language, which can have negative consequences for them and their peers. They may have to give up their own background in order to join the more prestigious target society. Their less determined peers may see this change as a betrayal, a reason not to follow their example.

The Learner

When we think about the language learners themselves, we need to keep several factors in mind. All students have diverse needs, backgrounds, and goals. With adolescent language learners, factors such as peer pressure and level of home support can strongly affect their desire and ability to learn a second language. Immigrant adolescents like those profiled in chapter 1 have additional factors related to the need to adjust to a new culture during a very difficult time in their lives (see Lucas, 1997).

Diverse needs and goals

A basic educational principle is that new learning has to be based on old learning, on prior experiences and existing skills. Although this principle is known and agreed upon by all educators, in practice it is often overshadowed in schools by the administrative convenience of the linear curriculum and the single textbook. Homogeneous curricula and materials are problematic enough if all learners are from a single language and cultural background, but they are indefensible given the great diversity in today's classrooms, which requires a different conception of curricula and a different approach to materials. Differentiation and individualization are not a luxury in this context. They are a necessity.

Learners not only differ in terms of their prior languages, they also have different goals and ambitions. Learners' goals may determine the ways they use the language being learned, how native-like their pronunciation will be, how lexically elaborate and grammatically accurate their utterances will be, and how much energy they will expend to understand messages in the target language.

Learners' goals in second language learning can vary from wholly integrative, the desire to assimilate and become a full member of the English-speaking world, to more instrumental, oriented toward specific goals such as academic or professional success. It is often assumed that an integrative orientation is more conducive to second language success than an instrumental one, though no conclusive evidence exists either way (Ellis, 1994; Gardner & Tremblay, 1994). What matters most is that students clarify their goals and then find clear and consistent ways of relating their second language learning experiences to those goals. For this to be possible, students must find meaningful opportunities to use the language and feel accepted and valued in the community.

Peer groups

Teenagers tend to be heavily influenced by their peer groups. In second language learning, peer pressure often undermines the goals that parents and teachers set in terms of language proficiency and attainment. In foreign language learning (e.g., French or Spanish), peer pressure often reduces the desire of the student to work toward a native-like accent, since the sounds of the target language may be regarded as "funny." In learners of English as a second language, speaking like a native speaker may unconsciously be regarded as a sign of no longer belonging to the peer group and may lead to rejection. In working with secondary school students, it is important to keep these peer influences in mind and, as much as possible, to foster a positive image for second language proficiency.

One solution to this problem is for teachers and other school personnel to stress that the acquisition of native-like proficiency in English does not mean losing one's peer-group dialect or street language. Everyone is capable of code switching, and indeed, to some extent everyone does code switch when moving in and out of different groups during work and leisure. The value of an ability to switch from standard English to the English of the adolescent community, and from English to the native language, or from the familiar register in the native language to its academic register, should be highlighted. In this way, the stigma that may be attached to speaking fluent English can be counteracted by a realization that communication needs in a new context do not need to undermine one's native language and cultural heritage. This is what the Spindlers (1993) referred to when they stated that requirements of the situated self should not impair the enduring self.

Home support

Support from home is very important for successful second language learning. As discussed earlier, this support may be provided in ways that are not visible to school personnel (Bhachu, 1985) and consequently may be misunderstood by them. Furthermore, some educators believe that support from home should take the form of speaking only English in the home (see, e.g., recommendations made in Rodríguez, 1982). However, far more important than speaking English is that parents value both the native language and English, communicate with their children in whichever language is most convenient, and show support for and interest in their children's progress.

For example, Gibson's study of Punjabi high school students in a Central Valley California community (1993) found that they did very well academically although they were not integrated into the larger school community. The students in her study did not participate in sports or after-school extracurricular activities because of their parents' encouragement to work hard on homework. In this case, parental expectations and belief in the importance of schooling had an impact on their children's persistence and seriousness in school. As one mother explained to Gibson, "the main thing is to study" (p. 118); their social life would come later, after their studies. By the same token, these teenagers, unlike their peers, did not take jobs after school because their parents believed that their job was to study.

In another study, Suárez-Orozco (1996) focused on Central American immigrant high school students, attempting to explain the school success many of them experienced "despite a school atmosphere of drugs, violence, low expectations, the calculated tracking of minority students into nonacademic subjects (in already nonacademic schools), bitter teachers, the seductive offers of more acculturated peers to join the street culture, and the need to work to help the family" (p. 132). Parents expressed that they had moved to this country, escaping political turmoil and wars, for the welfare of their children. They had left loved ones behind so that their children could become "somebody" tomorrow. The students had developed a dual frame of reference as they compared present opportunities in the host country and the reality of violence and poverty they had left at home. In their minds, there was no doubt that the situation here was preferable and promised a brighter future. If they worked hard, they would be able to repay their parents and others in their homeland for the sacrifices they had made. Their determination to compensate their parents with the fruits of schooling was so clear that teachers and others saw them as more eager to learn, exerting greater effort, studying harder, and consequently getting better grades than other minority students in their schools.

Role models

In addition to the previously mentioned social factors, role models, who usually come from outside the family, can have an impact. Students need to have positive and realistic role models who symbolize the value of additive bilingualism, the acquisition of a second language without concurrent loss of the first language. Ms. Baez, a teacher, was such a role model for Luis Rodríguez (see **Practices That Address Immigrant Students' Needs** in chapter 1 of this volume). It would also be appropriate for students to read literature about the personal experiences of people from diverse language and dialect backgrounds. Through discussions of the challenges experienced by others, they can develop a better understanding of their own.

Integrative and instrumental orientation

Learning a second language is different from learning other subject matter in school because language belongs to a person's whole social being, is part of a person's identity, and is used to convey this identity to others. Consequently, it has a significant effect on the social nature of the learner. This is why in order to understand students' success or lack of it in learning English, one of the variables to be considered is their attitudes toward the community of English speakers. Gardner's socioeducational model of language learning (1989)—posited for the study of foreign languages—distinguishes two orientations, integrative and instrumental. When learners study a language with the wish to identify with the culture of the speakers of a language, we have a case of integrative orientation. When they engage in learning the language to fulfill external goals such as reading a book, passing a test, or getting a job, the orientation is instrumental.

Acceptance and opportunities

Gardner's original distinction has been influential in the field, and some people have correlated an integrative orientation with success in the learning of other languages. Second language learning, however, does not take place in a vacuum, and therefore it is also important to study the context in which that learning takes place in order to better understand the complexities involved. In the case of English as a second language, it is essential to ask ourselves if the diverse communities surrounding students (the classroom, the school, the neighborhood, and the larger community) demonstrate acceptance of these students, support their efforts, and offer them genuine English-learning opportunities.

The Learning Process

When we think of second language development as a learning process, we need to remember that different students have different learning styles, that intrinsic motivation aids learning, and that the quality of classroom interaction matters a great deal.

Learning styles

Methods of second language teaching have generally assumed that all learners learn in identical ways. However, research has made it clear that there are great individual differences among learners in the ways they learn a second language (Skehan, 1989). Some of these differences can be grouped together as learning styles—cognitive, physical, and social preferences for certain ways of learning. Some learners may be more analytically oriented and thrive on picking apart words and sentences. Others may be more globally oriented, needing to experience overall patterns of language in meaningful contexts before being able to make sense of the linguistic parts and forms. Some learners are more visually oriented, others more geared to sounds; some require silence for study, while others prefer a busy and noisy environment. Some prefer to work on their own, and others work best in cooperative groups. Howard Gardner suggests that new concepts to be learned can be presented via at least five different entry points, which map onto the different intelligences of students: (a) the narrational entry point, (b) the logical-quantitative, (c) the fundational, (d) the aesthetic, and (e) the experiential (1991, p. 245).

Motivation

A crucial factor in successful learning is motivation, especially intrinsic motivation. According to Deci and Ryan (1985; see also Deci, 1995), intrinsic motivation refers to basic human needs for competence, autonomy, and relatedness. Intrinsically motivated activities are those that the learner engages in for their own sake because of their value, interest, and challenge to the learner. Such activities present the best possible opportunities for learning. Unfortunately, the high school environment contains many external threats, rewards, and controls related to learning, including an excessive focus on grades, tests, and behavioral discipline, all of which tend to undermine intrinsic motivation, to the detriment of students' progress (Csikszentmihalyi, Rathunde, & Whalen, 1993; Deci, 1995; Kohn, 1993).

Classroom interaction

An important variable in second language learning is the quality of classroom interaction. Language learning does not occur as a result of the transmission of facts about language or a succession of rote memorization drills, but rather as a result of opportunities for meaningful interaction with others in the target language. Therefore, lecturing and recitation are not the most appropriate modes of language use in the second language classroom. Instead, teachers need to move toward more richly interactive language use with their students, such as the instructional conversations described by Tharp and Gallimore (1988) and Goldenberg (1991) or collaborative classroom work (Adger, Kalyanpur, Peterson, & Bridger, 1995; Cohen, 1994). In chapter 4, I elaborate on the quality of teaching and classroom interaction necessary for the successful education of immigrant teenagers.

Expectations and support

Effective instruction for immigrant students should be guided by (1) high standards for learning, (2) a belief that second language learners can achieve them, and (3) knowledge of how to structure teaching and learning to support students in their gradual acquisition of sophisticated proficiencies. Although these read as common-sense educational notions, they are not often practiced in the education of immigrant students. It is a common experience for these students to be given materials (if available) produced for elementary school children, to be enrolled in courses that drill them and prepare them for participation in everyday life events instead of complex academic interactions, and in general to be made to feel as if they were ignorant children, instead of knowledgeable teenagers who have strengths that can be successfully built on to develop English and academic skills. In contrast, current theories of teaching and learning espouse the view that learning precedes development (Vygotsky, 1978) and works best when anchored in prior knowledge. These theories advocate classroom activity targeted just far enough ahead of students' conceptual and linguistic development to stretch their levels of competence.

Social and Cultural Contexts of Second Language Development

So far, I have discussed the second language acquisition process from the perspective of the language, the learner, and the learning process. But the picture is not complete without a fourth component that encompasses the other three. The larger social and cultural context of American society has a tremendous impact on second language learning, especially for immigrant students. The status of students' ethnic groups in relationship to the larger culture can help or hinder the desire to acquire the language of mainstream society. In addition, current views on immigration and immigrants affect these students and their experiences in American schools. As Spindler and Spindler (1993) argue, we must consider how the educational system contributes to increasing or decreasing the marginalization of immigrant students who enter the system with marginal status.

Most immigrant students are children of poverty and thus live in poor neighborhoods, sometimes sharing very limited space with other immigrant families. Youngsters in these situations occasionally end up spending more time in the streets than they would if they had more space at home or if they had access to neighborhood centers where they could spend their time safely and productively. In addition, gangs and violence are often part of the daily activities in many poor neighborhoods today so that, for these poor young men and women, a central feature of their social context is the presence of violence and gangs.

The social circumstances of minority education have been the subject of much study ever since the theories of racial and cultural deficits based on genetic differences among ethnic groups, as proposed by Jensen (1969) and others, were rejected. (That such theories have not completely disappeared is evidenced by the recent publication of Herrnstein and Murray's book *The Bell Curve* (1994) and the controversy it caused.) Early assumptions of cultural deprivation, that is, the notion that some groups are less successful because their cultural context does not stimulate the cognitive, linguistic, and emotional growth that is necessary for academic and social success, were soon challenged by theories of cultural difference (Foley, 1991; Ogbu, 1991). Cultural difference theories have brought into focus such issues as the relationships between different cultural practices, cross-cultural access to goods and services, and gaps between social groups and institutions. Instead of seeing a minority culture as the culprit, differential success (or access) is studied from the perspective of the dynamics between the groups and individuals involved. The most important question from this perspective is how groups, and individuals within these groups, interact with one another.

The success, or lack thereof, of certain minority groups in society and in education is the result of complex interactions of factors that emerge when subordinate groups come into contact with dominant (controlling) groups. These factors, which are not random but rather exhibit certain predictable patterns that can be studied, are discussed below.

Voluntary or Involuntary Status

One approach to the study of the social and cultural contexts of education is represented by the work of John Ogbu, who argues for the importance of historical and societal forces in explaining the educational success or lack of success of different minority groups. Ogbu, together with Maria Eugenia Matute-Bianchi (Ogbu, 1978; Ogbu & Matute-Bianchi, 1986), has developed a theoretical framework that classifies minority groups into involuntary (originally called "castelike"; see Foley, 1991, and Trueba, 1991, for a discussion on the problems with this term) and voluntary minorities. Involuntary (non-immigrant) minorities are those whose incorporation into the dominant society was the result of slavery, conquest, or colonization, as was the case with African Americans and Native Americans in the United States. Voluntary or immigrant minorities are those who moved to this country "because they believed that the move would lead to more economic well-being, better overall opportunities or greater political freedom" (Ogbu 1991, p. 8).

Ogbu makes a further distinction between primary and secondary cultural and language differences. Primary differences are those that existed before the groups in question came into contact; secondary differences emerged subsequent to contact. Ogbu associates the latter case primarily with involuntary minorities, who often develop an oppositional identity, based on their interpretations of discriminatory treatment, which is perceived as being institutionalized and enduring (Ogbu, 1991, p. 16). One element of this discrimination manifests itself as a job ceiling, or formal and informal practices that limit access to desirable jobs (Ogbu, 1991, p. 10).

Ogbu's framework is too general to be more than a point of departure in the study of immigrant students in secondary school. As Matute-Bianchi notes in her study of Mexican-descent students in central California, many students "do not fit neatly into either the immigrant or non-immigrant ethnic identification system" (Matute-Bianchi, 1991, pp. 210-11). In a sense, most, if not all, immigrant school children (and the children of immigrants) are involuntary minorities, since they almost invariably have not decided to live and study in this country, even though their families may have immigrated voluntarily (the most common exception to this may be foreign exchange students). Immigrant students' families may to varying degrees maintain pride in their primary culture and language, they may value education to a greater or lesser extent, and they may or may not have developed some form of oppositional identity. These differences are likely to have cognitive, emotional, and social consequences for the students' performance in school, but the degree to which this is the case can vary enormously from group to group and from one individual to another.

Some researchers have expanded Ogbu's framework to underscore the importance of race in immigrant students' experiences and perceptions of their opportunity to succeed in American society. In a study of Russian and Korean immigrant high school students in Los Angeles, Tuan (1995) found that although both groups of students associated primarily with students from their own country and were perceived by school authorities as displaying clannish attitudes, they were at the same time perceived as being high achievers, bound for college. The groups' school experiences and the strategies they employed to get to college, however, followed different paths. Korean students, as non-White immigrants, were discriminated against and excluded in ways that the Russian students, as White immigrants, were not. The Koreans, therefore, decided to study diligently, ignore attacks, and avoid confrontation.

The Russian students, on the other hand, did not feel the racial tensions of their Korean counterparts. At the same time, they had experienced their schools in Russia as being more advanced and demanding. Wanting to get a university education, they became impatient in high school and and found the academic content boring. Many 17- and 18-year-olds among them left high school and went directly into junior college (Tuan, 1995, p. 123). Both groups, then, successfully negotiated their way into postsecondary education. Tuan warned, however, that if Ogbu's framework were to be used to explain the Korean students' situation, an important subtlety might be missed. In Ogbu's terms, the Korean immigrant students would be classified as voluntary minorities because their families moved to the United States for economic reasons, and the possibility of returning home was open to them. According to Ogbu, immigrant voluntary minorities are inured to the psychological cost of discrimination. Tuan comments, however, that Koreans' experiences "suggest that concerns over racial exclusion and targeting may well be perceived as a lasting threat" (p. 126). If this is the case, it may be that non-White voluntary immigrant groups "end up adopting some of the same characteristics assigned to involuntary groups such as disenchantment with and rejection of the host society" (p. 127). For the most part, however, Korean immigrant students' strategies were adaptive and not oppositional.

Multiple Worlds, Multiple Transitions

Ann Phelan and her colleagues focused on the multiple boundaries that students must negotiate every day between the worlds of family, school, peers, and friends (Phelan, Davidson, & Cao, 1991), with their varying norms, values, beliefs, expectations, and actions. The study illuminates the difficulty that immigrant secondary school students experience when they cross worlds that are not congruent with each other and when success in school comes at the expense of negating family and old friends. For example, immigrant students may not let their parents know about school functions or meetings because they are embarrassed that their parents speak and behave in ways different from those expected in school, or they disassociate from their neighborhood friends or relatives because they are not school oriented. For some of these students, success is consciously negotiated by carefully studying the different groups in school and imitating certain behaviors to gain entry into those groups. The process illustrates the importance of developing accepting and nourishing climates in school, of understanding the tensions created by diverse worlds, and of helping students become aware of their options. Acceptance, however, is seldom complete; it may work in some classrooms, but not necessarily beyond them, and some teenagers may remain isolated within the school, in the neighborhood, and at home.

Alienation and Gangs

For many immigrant youngsters, there are practically no safe havens from the violence that plagues inner cities, small towns, and even rural areas. Increasingly, we see violence entering school campuses, making it less likely that schools can be perceived as safe zones for youth. If immigrant students find themselves rejected by teachers, school personnel, and classmates, they will look elsewhere for the trust and sense of belonging that is denied to them in school and other institutions (Heath & McLaughlin, 1993; Vigil, 1993). Milbrey McLaughlin and colleagues (McLaughlin, Irby, & Langman, 1994) studied the successful building of community that some neighborhood organizations have managed. They underscored the importance of youth organizations and activities that (1) are rooted in the local community and informed by local knowledge, (2) engage young people in shaping the organization and its tasks, and (3) view teenagers not as the problem, but as participants in and contributors to the solution. The staff who run these organizations reach, motivate, and work with youngsters whom many dismiss as irredeemable or useless. Key qualities of these "wizards"—a term applied to the successful neighborhood organizers because "they have succeeded where so many have not" (p. xvii)—are a love for young people, a strong sense of mission, indefatigable commitment to their work, and a passion for the organization's chief activity, such as drama or athletics. There is a desperate need for urban sanctuaries of the kind described in this book, where teenagers can feel comfortable, safe, positively engaged, and challenged by welcoming others.

Alienation is not only felt in schools and communities. At times, immigration and adaptation to a hostile and complex environment have so completely disrupted family life and traditional values that home can no longer provide a place of security and affiliation. Under these circumstances, the only security for some immigrant teenagers, such as the Vietnamese boys and girls that Vigil (1988) studied, comes from a gang. Since no single factor—economics, family breakdown, the historical dimensions of an individual's or a cohort's life, social control, and so on—can by itself explain gang participation, Vigil elaborated a multiple marginality framework. This framework integrates most of the elements that have been used previously to explain gang behavior and is also used to analyze individual cases of teenagers in gangs, including immigrant youth.

Not all troubled immigrant teenagers turn to gangs, though, and some enter mainstream society partially and at will. Thus, it remains important to treat immigrant students as individual cases, although the forces that trigger their behavior, such as societal stratification, can be studied systematically.

The presence of gangs does not affect only students. Teachers of immigrant students also feel the impact of violence in school and are often faced with very difficult situations that are beyond their power to address. Susan Katz Weinberg (1994) tells the story of Elvin, a 15-year-old Latino student in her seventh-grade ESL class who confessed that he had participated in some drive-by shootings. His trust in her put her in an ethically complex situation.

One day in late September, he pulled out his gun to show me. Shocked, I was very torn about what to do. Elvin trusted me. If I reported him, he would get expelled and only be out in the streets even more. If I did not report him, I would be delivering the message that I condoned the possession of guns at school. After hours of internal struggle, I finally reported his action to the vice principal, and Elvin was expelled the next day. Expelled to nowhere. He hasn't been to school since. (p. 2)

Gangs, alienation, low social status, and prejudice are all part of the new world that many immigrant, non-White students face. These issues shape their educational experiences in complex ways that teachers need to understand if they are to teach them well.

Negative Attitudes Toward Immigrants

Another very serious issue that immigrant students face is negative public perceptions and the increasing intolerance in this country for the presence of certain immigrant groups. In the current public debate about immigration and bilingualism, one often hears people say that there is a difference between the old wave of immigrants to the United States and the more recent one. In these people's perceptions, the former immigrants assimilated to American culture and the English language quite rapidly and were thus able to advance themselves, while more recent immigrants hold on to their culture and languages, do not learn English, and consequently do not succeed in society. In order to address this belief, it is important to analyze its development historically, economically, and politically within the changing context of contemporary American schooling (see also Wiley, 1996, for discussion).

While the unofficial U.S. language policy has fluctuated between periods of greater or lesser tolerance for the use of many languages, every immigrant group that has settled in this country has spoken English by the third generation (Pease-Alvarez & Hakuta, 1993; Veldman, 1983). If anything, the current shift from the immigrant language to English is accelerating and is achieved in two, and sometimes one generation (Hakuta & D'Andrea, 1992). Even though U.S. language policies have not been consistent, a selective memory of the past has remained constant.

The first attempt to document the differences between "new" and "old" immigrants occurred in 1911, when the Dillingham Commission (described in Hakuta, 1986, p. 16), after 4 years of study, produced a 42-volume report that appeared to legitimize the fear that Italians, Jews, Greeks, and Slavs—unlike their German, Scandinavian, and Irish predecessors—preferred to isolate themselves from native-born Americans and older immigrants, a preference that resulted in their failure to assimilate and perpetuated their poverty. The report also noted these groups' "backwardness" in the acquisition of English. As Hakuta documents, the Commission paid little attention to its own data. In making comparisons among groups, they did not consider the length of time that the different immigrant groups had had to settle in this country. Had this comparison been included, the findings would have shown that new immigrants follow the same patterns as previous immigrant groups. But the report drew a line between "old" immigrants from northern Europe (most of whom had arrived before the early 1880s and assimilated rapidly) and "new" immigrants (poor, unskilled, and ghettoized) to whom all kinds of negative qualities were attributed. The Dillingham report, although full of interpretive errors, helped to perpetuate negative stereotypes and divisions under the guise of a serious study. Once the problem was identified, a solution could be proposed: The "Americanization" campaign began. Philanthropists working through organizations such as the YMCA launched efforts to teach adult immigrants the English language and the American values of free enterprise. Business leaders joined this crusade after a worker's strike was coordinated in Lawrence, Massachusetts, in which more than 20 languages were used by the strikers (Crawford, 1989). The strike seemed to offer proof that multilingualism and nonassimilation can cause political unrest and economic suffering.

A strong link between English proficiency and political loyalty had been forged in the United States, and it was felt that if an immigrant did not speak English, he was probably a traitor to his new country. In 1915, the National Americanization Committee started a project called "English First" in Detroit, with the support of the local Board of Commerce (Crawford, 1989, p. 26). Employers required that foreign-born workers attend Americanization classes to promote the assimilation of new arrivals into American culture and the English language, giving up their own language and culture in the process. At the same time, it was suggested that the immigration of southern and central Europeans should be restricted by the establishment of control over the flow of immigrants (Kamin, 1974).

In similar fashion, today we see a resurgence of the issues of positive "old" versus negative "new" migratory waves, calls for the restriction of certain types of immigration, and the idea that English should be the "glue that holds the country together" (Roth, 1995). Once again, despite evidence that new generations of immigrants are learning English more rapidly than at any other time in American history, the perceived failure of immigrant groups to learn the English language reflects larger racial, economic, and political concerns.

Structural Obstacles That Inhibit Students' Success

A s organizations, American high schools do not represent unitary, coherent, well-articulated contexts for learning, but "multiple embedded contexts that define the secondary school workplace and shape teaching and learning within them" (McLaughlin & Talbert, 1990, p. 7). Several characteristics of most U.S. high schools create barriers to the success of immigrant students: the division of the school day into short class periods, the separation of school subjects into different departments, the practice of tracking, the practice of placing students of the same age in the same grade regardless of previous educational preparation, and the use of traditional methods of documenting student achievement. These practices can cause a number of problems for immigrant students, who may get lost between the cracks of this divided system or who may consistently be placed in low academic tracks, below their potential level of performance.

Fragmented School Days

For most immigrant students, secondary schooling in their home countries is a much more integrated experience than it is in the United States. In many countries, students in secondary schools are typically grouped as cohorts who remain together for their educational experience and seldom change classrooms, except for laboratory work. It is the teachers who move from one classroom to another to teach different subjects and different groups of students. As a consequence, most foreign-born students come from secondary schools in which they identified themselves with a particular group of peers and even a particular room, and where they developed a strong sense of community. In U.S. secondary schools, the continuous movement from class to class in an unfamiliar building and the constant shift from one group of classmates to another increases immigrant students' sense of confusion and alienation, making it difficult for them to find an anchor in a consistent group of friends and teachers on whom they can rely.

In other educational systems, daily class schedules are based on the relative importance of subjects, rather than on an evenly distributed time allocation for each class. For example, a Peruvian secondary school student's schedule might include 2 hours of mathematics (typically scheduled in the morning to emphasize its importance), 1 hour of language arts (Spanish language and literature), 2 hours of science, 1 hour of philosophy, and 1 hour of civics. On Tuesdays and Thursdays, there would be two 1-hour periods of language arts, 1 hour of Peruvian history, 1 hour of world history, 2 hours of foreign language, 1 hour of art, and 1 hour of physical education. Thus, in their home countries, secondary school students might take more than six courses per semester that vary in length, demand, and relative prestige. As newcomers to the United States, students are often surprised that the ninth-grade physical education class receives as much time daily as the mathematics class, and that they will enroll in six courses of 50 minutes each or, in some cases, seven classes of even shorter duration.

As a result of the movement to restructure schools to improve the education of all students, new schedule formats such as block scheduling have been created that provide longer stretches of time for classes. Block scheduling can be immensely helpful in the education of immigrant secondary school students, because it allows teachers and students to take the time to pursue in depth the kinds of knowledge that are critical and relevant for all students. However, block scheduling needs to be carefully planned around the needs of English language learners to ensure that it is used to advance their academic, cognitive, and linguistic development (see Olsen & Jaramillo, in press). Effective block scheduling requires new ways of conceptualizing instruction. It does not suffice to stretch the same lesson over double the time, or to say, like the teacher in Elmore's article (1995), "Oh good, now I can show the whole movie."

Departmentalized Schools

In secondary schools in the United States, separate departments constitute organizational sub-units "within which different educational structures and processes, collegial relations and organizational cultures can be established" (McLaughlin & Talbert, 1990, p. 7). Whereas elementary school departments and subjects are relatively undifferentiated, in public and private middle and high schools, each department has its own personality, modus operandi, and reputation, and teachers often do not interact across departments (Johnson, 1990).

While elementary school teachers consider themselves generalists, secondary school teachers think of themselves as subject matter experts. Yet for second language learners, it is helpful if a teacher makes connections across ideas and disciplines. Most subject matter teachers do not have this experience. Furthermore, secondary school teachers expect their students to be competent readers and writers. Unless they teach English, they typically do not consider the teaching of reading and writing skills to be part of their work, nor do they feel prepared to do it. Many immigrant students need to develop the skills to become critical readers and writers within specific subject areas (and to transfer to English the skills that they possess in their own language in these fields), and they need teachers who are able to help them do this.

In some secondary school departments, teachers gain rights by virtue of their seniority, such as the right to teach the most coveted courses. Consequently, courses considered to be desirable—such as college preparatory or advanced placement courses—are assigned to teachers who have been in the department the longest. This leaves the new, inexperienced teachers with the courses that are considered most difficult to teach. This arrangement may benefit the experienced teachers, but it negatively affects immigrant students because classes with newcomers and English language learners typically become the responsibility of teachers who are new to teaching. A considerable amount of teachers' pedagogical knowledge develops as a result of reflective practice and participation in professional development while teaching (González & Darling-Hammond, 1997). This means that new teachers have limited abilities to meet the needs of immigrant students. The mismatch between students' needs and teachers' abilities is not beneficial for either.

Furthermore, in schools with strong departmental boundaries, there are no clearly established responsibilities for the education of students who need to develop academic expertise and facility in English at the same time. Individual teachers who are overwhelmed by working every day with five groups of 35 energetic teenagers who bring many life problems to school do not have the time or energy to take on another major responsibility without the infrastructure to support it. Thus, many secondary school teachers are reluctant to expand their expertise and learn how to teach their subject matter to second language learners.

In departmentalized secondary schools, ESL components are usually created in English departments with the goal of developing immigrant students' skills in English. These subunits, however, do not work well in most places. As a California program director declared, "ESL is the stepchild of the English department. It has less status, fewer resources, and is given lower priority than 'regular' English classes" (META, 1995, p. 57). These courses end up being "the school's inner ghetto" (Suárez-Orozco, 1989, p. 133), and the teachers who teach them often feel inferior to other teachers. As one teacher in Suárez-Orozco's study commented, "They think we can't teach anything else, and that's why we go into bilingual" (p. 134).

Content classes taught in students' primary languages or in sheltered English are typically the responsibility of subject area departments. In schools where the needs of English language learners are central to the educational activities of these departments, this arrangement works well because it allows teachers to set the same standards for all subject matter classes, regardless of whether they are mainstream, sheltered, or taught in students' primary languages. However, departments that consistently place the needs of English language learners at the core of their concerns are rare. What typically happens is that sheltered courses (which are supposed to cover mainstream curricula using texts with special pedagogical accommodations for English learners) and subject matter courses taught in students' native languages are considered watered-down versions of the demanding regular courses. In addition, classes are offered without the support of appropriate materials, classes are crowded (for example, a class might start with 32 students, but every new immigrant student that arrives throughout the year is added to it), or students with limited prior schooling and low literacy skills are placed in the same class with students who can read adequately in the subject area.

The power that department chairs have over curricula at the high school level can also create problems for immigrant students, if the chairperson is not interested in attending to the students' needs. In a study of 15 California secondary schools with exemplary programs for immigrant students, the researchers found one school in which "one department chair refuses to offer advanced classes for L.E.P. students even when there is a trained and willing staff member to teach the class" (META, 1995, p. 57). In another study of immigrant students in California's secondary schools, researchers stressed the danger of having department chairs create courses in their departments when they have no commitment to or knowledge about the education of second language learners (Minicucci & Olsen, 1992).

As a result of recent interest in more integrated teaching, some secondary schools, especially middle schools, have started organizing around "houses" or multidisciplinary clusters of teachers who share the same two or three groups of students. These new ways of structuring teaching and learning hold promise for English language learners because the focus is on understanding major themes that connect various disciplines. At the same time, interdisciplinary teaming and curriculum development require a great deal of time and energy. Teachers need time to meet and work collaboratively.

Another response to the concerns described above is to create a separate ESL department that is not a unit within the English department and which is responsible for teaching English language development (ELD) classes and for coordinating all of the classes for immigrant students. This arrangement is less common than subject departmentalization, however. In the META (1995) study of California schools mentioned above, only 2 out of 15 schools had a separate ESL/ELD department. Teachers in these departments felt that the arrangement worked better for their students and for themselves, because it conferred on their department a status equal to that of other departments.

Having a separate ESL department is particularly appealing in schools in which ESL teachers have already acquired a respected status. At El Sausal Middle School in Salinas, California, for example, some of the most senior and accomplished teachers work in the ESL department. This enhances the programs within the department and has a positive effect on the students. However, when ESL teachers do not have an established reputation, the arrangement may further alienate populations that are already marginal. In fact, many ESL departments and classes are housed in back of schools, in portable classrooms, and even in closets. In a study of mainstream departments in high schools, Susan Moore Johnson (1990) concluded, "There is some evidence from the present study that teachers working in strong departments enjoy a greater sense of influence and efficacy than do those whose departments are low in status and resources" (p. 182). When ESL or bilingual departments have low status in a school, other signs of marginality emerge as well, such as lack of books and other materials and limited participation by students in extra-curricular activities, student government, or other significant aspects of the life of the school. A separate ESL department may promote recognition of the needs of its students, but its existence can also perpetuate the perception that English language learners are the exclusive responsibility of a few teachers. A more desirable solution is to work toward the recognition that the education of immigrant minorities is the responsibility of everyone at the school and of the community at large.

A Complex and Tracked System of Courses

High schools in the United States have a complex system of courses and requirements that sometimes even members of the native English-speaking population know little about. For a student coming from a different educational system, a different language, and a different culture, this complexity is difficult to grasp and negotiate. A specific number of credits and courses are required for high school graduation. If a student is interested in attending a 4-year postsecondary institution, a certain combination of classes must be taken as well. Frequently, immigrant students in the 12th grade find out very close to graduation that they do not have the credits needed to graduate. Often, their teachers do not know what they need, either. In a recent informal poll that I conducted of 20 teachers in a high school in California, only 2 could explain the California university system's admission requirements. Clearly, teachers need to be informed of these requirements so they can help their students. Students and their relatives need to be told, in their own language and in simple terms, the courses required to graduate from high school, as well as the courses needed to go to a university. Clear ways of keeping track of students' advancement toward graduation should also be developed, and students and their parents should receive reports every semester describing the students' progress.

Another feature of U.S. secondary schools that makes it difficult for English language learners to succeed is the sorting of students based on teachers' perceptions of their academic capabilities, an institutionalized practice of ability grouping called "tracking" (Oakes, 1985). Once divided, students are often treated in ways that are consistent with these estimations, and a self-fulfilling cycle is created in which those selected for the more challenging courses rise to the challenge, and those condemned to the lower level tracks perform less well, consequently legitimating their placement.

Immigrant students are overrepresented in lower track courses (Harklau, 1994), which do not provide them with what the University of California calls the "A-F requirements" needed to apply to institutions in its system (Vigil, 1988). The courses required for undergraduate admission also vary with each institution, making the situation even more complex for immigrant students. Table 2 compares admission requirements for the University of California and the California State University systems.

Table 2. Courses Required for University Admission in California

Courses	University of California "A–F" requirements	California State University requirements
History/ social sciences	A) 2 years of U.S. history or 1/2 year of U.S. history and 1/2 year of civics or American government; 1 year of world history, cultures, and geography	1 year of U.S. history or U.S. history and government
English	B) 4 years of college preparatory English that includes frequent and regular writing and reading of classic and modern literature. Not more than 2 semesters of ninth grade English can be used to meet this requirement.	4 years
Mathematics	C) 3 years required, 4 recommended, of college preparatory math that includes the topics covered in elementary and advanced algebra and two- and three-dimensional geometry	3 years of algebra, geometry, or intermediate algebra
Laboratory science	D) 2 years required, 3 recommended, of biology, chemistry, or physics	1 year of biology, chemistry, physics or other acceptable laboratory science
Language other than English	E) 2 years required, 3 recommended. Courses should emphasize speaking and understanding and include instruction in grammar, vocabulary, reading, and composition.	2 years
College preparatory electives	F) 2 years required; 4 semesters in addition to those required in A–E above, chosen from visual and performing arts, history, social science, English, advanced math, laboratory science, and language other than English	3 years, selected from English, advanced math, social science, history, laboratory science, foreign language, visual and performing arts, agriculture
Visual and performing arts		1 year art, dance, drama, theater, or music
Grades required	Grade point average defined by the scholarship requirement: If 3.3 or higher, minimum requirement for admission is met; if below 3.3 but above 2.81, minimum requirement is met only if certain scores are attained in the SAT.	"C" or better for each of the courses

Note. The data in column 2 are from *Introducing the University,* 1996, Oakland, CA: The University of California, Student Academic Services. The data in column 3 are from *Undergraduate Admission,* 1996, Long Beach, CA: The California State University.

The experience of Chuy (a pseudonym) illustrates a pattern common among immigrant students learning English in California high schools. His senior year social studies teacher thought him an excellent university candidate. In her class he had been hard working, responsible, involved, and an able critical appraiser of situations. To their surprise and chagrin, Chuy's high school transcript (see Figure 1) revealed that he lacked the requisite coursework to qualify for university admission.

Although he had taken 8 semesters of math, none of them counted for university admission because all of them were different versions of basic, non-college-preparatory math, under different names: General Math, Survey Math, Business Math, Consumer Math, and General Math again. In fact, Chuy had taken 2 basic math courses in the same semester in 1995—Business Math and Consumer Math. He had taken 4 semesters of science, none of which counted for college application. He needed 2 semesters of laboratory science, but the courses he took did not have a lab. He had taken 20 English courses, only 2 of which were accepted (all were ESL or remedial courses, and only 2 count in the California State University system). He had taken 6 social studies courses, none of which qualified because he needed to have a minimum grade of C in a U.S. History class.

Chuy's case raises a number of questions. Who had scheduled him into these courses? Was he aware of the future they would determine for him? Could he have taken courses that would make it possible for him to apply to the university? How excited can a student be about taking the same low-level course eight times? Is Chuy's case an exception, or does this transcript represent a common pattern among immigrant students learning English? Chuy went on to graduate from high school, painfully aware that his high school education did not amount to much, although it could have been different.

```
_____ H I G H  S C H O O L                          11/26/96
STUDENT TRANSCRIPT
NAME:                              STU#:                    BIRTHDATE:
ADDRESS:                                                    SEX: M    GRADE: 12
PRIMARY GUARDIAN:
BIRTH PLACE:                       ENTER DATE:              LEAVE DATE:
```

GRD	DATE	COURSE-TITLE	MARK	CRED	GRD	DATE	COURSE-TITLE	MARK	CRED
09	11/92	--[SCHOOL NAME]			11	6/95	DRIVER ED	P	5.00
		ESL 1-AB	C	5.00			STORIES YTH T	D	5.00
		ESL 1-AB	C	5.00			ESL 3B		5.00
		GEN MATH SP	B	5.00			CHECK/CASH	C	5.00
		EARTH S G SP	C	5.00	11	7/95	GR WRITING	B	5.00
		SPAN 3-4 NS P	A	5.00	11	7/95	--		
		PHYS ED	A	2.00			GR WRITING	A	5.00
09	1/93	ESL 1-AB	B	5.00	11	8/95	--OUT OF DISTRICT SCHOOL		
		ESL 1-AB	B	5.00			ESL 3A	C	5.00
		GEN MATH SP	B	5.00	12	11/95	[SCHOOL NAME]		
		EARTH S G SP	C	5.00			SPAN 5-6 P NS	C	5.00
		SPAN 3-4 NS P	B	5.00			ENG 3-4 TR P	B-	5.00
		PHYS ED	B	5.00			AUTO S/MECH B1	C+	5.00
10	11/93	--[SCHOOL NAME]			12	1/96	SPAN 5-6 P NS	C	5.00
		ESL 2	B	5.00			ENG 3-4 TR P	D-	5.00
		ESL 2	B	5.00			AUTO S/MECH B1	C	5.00
		W HST/G P SHL	C	5.00	12	3/96	GR MATH	P	5.00
		SURV MATH SHL	D	5.00			US HIST P TR	D	5.00
		LIFE SCI SHL	D	5.00			PHYS ED	A	5.00*
		PHYS ED	B	5.00	12	6/96	CONS MATH G	B	5.00
10	1/94	ESL 2	B	5.00			US HIST P TR	D	5.00
		ESL 2	B	5.00			PHYS ED	A-	5.00*
		W HST/G P SHL	F	0.00					
		SURV MATH SHL	F	0.00					
		LIFE SCI SHL	D	5.00					
		PHYS ED	C	3.00					
		ELD 3	C	10.00					
11	11/94	--[SCHOOL NAME]							
		BUS MATH	F	0.00					
		ESL 3A	C	5.00					
		US HIST P SHL	F	0.00					
11	1/95	BUS MATH	F	0.00					
		ESL 3A	C	5.00					
		CON MATH	C	5.00					
		US HIST P SHL	D	5.00					
11	3/95	HEALTH ED SHL	B	5.00					
		STORIES YOUTH T	D	5.00					
		ESL 3B		5.00					
		CHECK/CASH	C	5.00					

```
LEGEND FOR WEIGHTED GPA: A=ADVANCED PLACEMENT, G=GATE, H=HONORS. COURSES NOT CALCULATED
IN GPA: *=PE, R=REPEATED, ROTC AND OTHER NON-ACADEMIC CLASSES.
****************************************************************************************
* CREDIT ATTEMPTED:  275.00      CREDIT COMPLETED:   250.00          CLASS SIZE: 429 *
* UNWEIGHTED GPA:       2.01     CAL-GRANT (10-11) GPA:  1.75    WEIGHTED GPA: 2.01 *
* UNWEIGHTED RANK:       264                                     WEIGHTED RANK: 264 *
```

Note. GR WRITING = General Writing, a low-level mainstream English course. ENG TR = English Transitional class, equivalent to a sheltered English class.

Figure 1. High school transcript of an immigrant student

Many secondary school counselors equate limited proficiency in English with academic limitations and act as gatekeepers to the more challenging academic credit-bearing courses that would give students more postsecondary options. Immigrant students are often scheduled into vocational courses such as woodshop or metals, and away from more creative, artistic, and professional options. While counselors are overtaxed in almost all secondary schools, the horror stories of students who are systematically placed in low-track classes, in spite of their abilities or interests, are a result of more than just counselor overwork. Ignorance and racism also play a part.

Luis Rodríguez (1993) remembers the inequities he had to suffer in schools in Los Angeles:

Friction filled [Mark Keppel High School's] hallways. The Anglo and Asian upper-class students from Monterey Park and Alhambra attended the school. They were tracked into the "A" classes; they were in the school clubs, they were the varsity team members and letter men. They were the pep squads and cheerleaders.

But the school also took in the people from the hills and surrounding community who somehow made it past junior high. They were mostly Mexican, in the "C" track (what they called the "stupid" classes), and who made up the rosters of the wood, print and auto shops. Only a few of these students participated in school government, in sports, or in the various clubs. (p. 83)

The opportunity for me to learn something new became an incentive for attending Taft High School. At Keppel and Continuation, I mainly had industrial art classes. So I applied for classes which stirred a little curiosity: photography, advanced art, and literature. The first day of school, a Taft High School counselor called me into her office.

"I'm sorry, young man, but the classes you chose are filled up," she said.

"What do you mean? Isn't there any way I can get into any of them?"

"I don't believe so. Besides, your transcripts show you're not academically prepared for your choices. These classes are privileges for those who have maintained the proper grades in the required courses. And I must add, you've obtained most of what credits you do have in industrial-related courses."

"I had to—that's all they'd give me," I said. "I just thought, maybe, I can do something else here. It seems like a good school and I want a chance to do something other than with my hands."

"It doesn't work that way," she replied. "I think you'll find our industrial arts subjects more suited to your needs."

I shifted in my seat and looked out the window. "Whatever." (pp. 136-137)

The great majority of immigrant students placed in low-track classes become trapped in them throughout their schooling, and are blamed for not having deserved the privilege of performing to high standards, as was the case with Luis Rodríguez. At other times, students who earned high grades in their home countries are sent to classes for students with learning difficulties, simply because they do not speak English well upon arrival (see Santiago, 1994). Some immigrant students in American middle schools are placed in low-track classes as they move into high school (Gándara, 1995). Parents' inability to speak English and help their children negotiate the school system compounds the problem (Gibson, 1995; Olsen, 1995).

Some English learners do develop an understanding of the tracking system on their own and learn what it takes to move to more challenging academic experiences offered by high-track classes. These students can achieve track crossings that even their native-born peers cannot accomplish. Linda Harklau (1994) studied four Chinese immigrant students in a California Central Coast high school. Two of the students in her case studies were able to move into the advanced placement classes, while the other two, although desiring to do the same, could not accomplish the move. The first two students' success resulted from their realization, soon after they entered the high school, that the school had a differentiated system of courses. This was not easy, since the tracking process was not transparent, but rather implicit and "almost covert" (p. 233). The students followed their hunches with conscious study of the teaching and expectations in different courses and applied their knowledge in strategic efforts to change tracks. They learned which adults in the school made the crucial decisions and on what basis, and they got them on their side, an amazing feat for second language learners.

It is not surprising, therefore, that most students attempting to "untrack" themselves are met with failure. The two failed students in Harklau's study had fatally miscalculated their counselor's assessment of their abilities.

Because Mr. Daniels did not share the brothers' estimation of their own academic ability, and regarded their ambitions as "unrealistic," he continually blocked their attempts to move up, despite their explicit desires to the contrary (and their mother's call supporting their request). Thus, simply expressing the desire to be in higher tracks, or even parental intervention, was not enough to be placed in higher classes; students had to actively negotiate perceptions of ability with school personnel, and convince at least one representative of the institution that they were "worthy" of being moved up. (p. 235)

When movement is possible, it may be aided by the "model minority" stereotype, through which Asian immigrants are seen as hard-working, ambitious, and well behaved (Suzuki, 1983; Wong, 1980; Wong, 1987). This stereotype, however, does not apply in all cases, as the previous example demonstrates. When the stereotype of a group is negative, then the negotiation of track boundaries becomes almost universally insurmountable.

The different treatment that students receive in high- and low-track classes reinforces the initial assessment and expectations of them when they were tracked. In her study, Harklau (1994) demonstrates that the types of academic work in which students engaged in the higher tracks developed in them the ability to engage in critical thinking and sustained arguments and to write extended pieces that were typically responded to and revised several times. Students' ability to learn and use the academic discourse of various disciplines was enhanced in these tracks. The way that writing, one of the most difficult areas for second language learners to conquer, was taught in the two tracks in Harklau's study illustrates the differences. The immigrant students tracked into the low-level classes were seldom given writing assignments. When they were, the assignments focused on writing disconnected sentences using one grammatical element. These assignments were returned with either a stamp saying "checked" or with superficial corrections of the mechanics of the language. Immigrant students in the advanced placement classes, however, were asked to reflect on readings by interpreting, hypothesizing, and analyzing characters and events. Thus, those students perceived as more capable had the opportunity to develop their linguistic and cognitive potential, and those perceived as less capable were treated as intellectual and linguistic paupers.

To address the tracking situation, some programs prepare linguistic and cultural minority students to meet the tougher challenges and master the selection process of a tracked system. These programs recognize that one of the reasons that immigrant students and English language learners are left out of higher level classes is that their own parents do not possess the cultural capital needed—the knowledge valued in school and an understanding of how the school system works—to socialize their children into the system and help them navigate it successfully. As Bernstein (1972), Heath (1986), and others have demonstrated, success in school depends on the ability to use language in ways that are different from everyday communication among relatives and friends. Middle- and upper-class children, who typically have well-educated parents, are socialized into the ways of using language that will help them succeed in school, and they are comfortable with the language of school. Children who do not develop academic language and norms at home cannot learn them intuitively, simply by attending class all day. Instead, they need to be taught explicitly (Delpit, 1995).

The Achievement Via Individual Determination (AVID) program, initiated in San Diego, California, by Mary Catherine Swanson, capitalizes on the idea of explicitly teaching to minority students and immigrant youth the norms for succeeding academically. AVID has now successfully spread throughout California and to other parts of the country. AVID staff recruit minority students enrolled in middle and high schools who are underachieving, to motivate and prepare them to perform well in advanced classes and to seek a college education (Mehan, Hubbard, Lintz, & Villanueva, 1994). They do so by enrolling students for 3 consecutive years in an AVID course taught daily at their schools as part of their regular schedule. Youngsters chosen to participate are "high potential/low performance" students (p. 2) who have a C average and whose parents have agreed to support their participation by signing a letter of commitment. AVID uses three strategies as cornerstones of the program: a heavy reliance on varied and intensive forms of writing, strategic development of the inquiry method to foster students' autonomy, and collaboration carried out in many ways and with many different participants. AVID is a very intensive program: 2 days a week are dedicated to writing and critical note-taking; for 2 days a week, students in small groups discuss with trained tutors from the community (usually students from a local college) questions they generated from their notes. The role of the tutor is not to provide answers to students' questions, but to help students clarify their thoughts based on their own questions. Once a week, the class is "motivational," devoted to outside speakers or to field trips to colleges.

The record achieved by AVID is impressive. It has had a positive impact on the lives of many immigrant students since 1992, when AVID staff began conducting courses in sheltered content instruction for immigrant secondary school students in the process of learning English. In a follow-up study of 248 students who fully participated in the program, 48% were enrolled in 4-year colleges, and 40% attended 2-year institutions. The positive impact was felt even on students who only participated for a year; 34% went on to a university after graduating from high school (Mehan, Hubbard, Lintz, & Villanueva, 1994). These results are important because, at a time when the number of jobs that require a college education is increasing, the number of students who do not attend college is also increasing, particularly among immigrants. While AVID does not dismantle the system of tracking, it "untracks" it for a group of students, assisting them to move into high-level courses and higher education. As·Mehan and his colleagues suggest (1994, p. 17), this untracking process may have the potential to be the first step in a true detracking effort.

Age–Grade Inflexibility

American schools assume that by the time students are 15 years old they should be enrolled in 9th or 10th grade and should have covered a certain amount of specified curriculum. Schools and teachers count on students being prepared for the courses they offer and assume a common baseline of content and skills possessed by all students of a given age. It is difficult to sustain this assumption with native-born, English-speaking teenagers; it is impossible with immigrant teenagers.

In some cases, the academic preparation that immigrant students bring to school is more sophisticated than that of their American counterparts. In the former Soviet Union, for example, students typically graduate from high school at the age of 16. Their schooling is more rigorous, accelerated, and demanding. The school experience for Russian students comprises 10 years, 2 years fewer than in the United States. In Form 5 (the equivalent of fifth grade), students study biology and geography; in Form 6 they study physics; and in Form 7 they study chemistry and trigonometry (Kashin, 1988). This excellent preparation helps them with school subjects in the United States because the topics covered are usually well known to them (with the exception of American history and government, which are often their most difficult courses). It may be advisable for a 17-year-old student in this situation to attend a community college or a university instead of enrolling in high school.

However, as the profiles of immigrant students in chapter 1 showed, the level and quality of schooling that immigrant students bring to school fluctuates greatly. Students who are nonliterate or who have had limited prior schooling need to work on the development of their literacy skills before they are scheduled into age-appropriate, grade-level subject matter classes. For these students, the commonly held belief in a linear progression of skills and an inflexible school schedule needs to change. Some school systems *are* flexible. As long as students want to stay in high school, they are allowed to stay beyond the prescribed high school age. These accommodations, however, are informal and sporadic. It may be beneficial to formalize these options for immigrant students.

Flexibility to accommodate students' differing educational backgrounds and English language and literacy levels needs to extend beyond school schedules and class assignments to include instruction. For example, teaching literacy to teenagers is very different from teaching initial literacy to children. To adapt a phrase that Paolo Freire popularized, teenagers know how to read the world; they now need to read the word (Freire & Macedo, 1987). Rather than working only with published texts, adolescent students can create texts from their own lives, which can generate critical discussions and further texts. Freire and Macedo call this approach *critical pedagogy*. A similar approach, without the emphasis on the co-construction of a critical consciousness, is called the Language Experience Approach in the United States (Dixon & Nessel, 1983). This approach has been used primarily with elementary school children, but it can also be used effectively with adolescents and adults (see Taylor, 1993).

Initial literacy must be developed in a language that the student understands because it is not possible to learn to read and write for the first time in a language that does not make any sense to the learner. It is not always possible, however, to find teachers who know the students' mother tongue well enough to develop their literacy in that language. In such cases, students need to develop some oral fluency in English first—with challenging, stimulating, and relevant topics—and then work on their literacy skills. We have very limited knowledge of how to develop initial literacy with middle and high school students. Some interesting projects have been developed for adults in Massachusetts by Paolo Freire and Donaldo Macedo (1987), which can serve as a model for the education of low-literate teenagers.

A program specifically designed to address the needs of immigrant students with limited prior schooling and low literacy skills is the New Beginnings program in Dade County, Florida (see also McDonnell & Hill, 1993). This 1-year program is designed to serve middle school-age students with literacy skills below the third grade level and high school-age students with literacy skills below the fifth grade level.

New Beginnings is located at schools that have enough students to form a class. If a school does not have enough students to have its own program, then students are bussed to a central location. The program focuses on the teaching of English to speakers of other languages (ESOL) and bilingual curriculum content (BCC) in Haitian Creole and Spanish. Emphasis is placed on the development of social and academic skills to enable students to succeed, first in the bilingual program and eventually in the mainstream curriculum. The goal is to offer underschooled and low-literate immigrant teenagers a safe haven in which to learn the strategies that will make them successful in the mainstream instead of failing or dropping out of school.

Teachers in New Beginnings are carefully selected for their commitment to educating immigrant students. When I visited five schools housing the program in May of 1995, I was impressed by the climate of support and cooperation that the teachers had established in their classrooms. I had extended conversations with the students, who were thankful that they did not have to go to regular classes immediately (it was difficult enough for them during breaks, when they were sometimes made fun of) and who felt nourished and challenged in their classes. Students' favorite part of the program was the TALL–ESOL component, Technology-Assisted Language Learning, which uses a combination of computer and noncomputer activities to develop students' social and academic skills in English. TALL–ESOL is part of a daily 2-period ESOL class. That class plus 1 period of civics, 2 of mathematics, and an elective form the middle school curriculum. High school-age students take 2 periods of ESOL, a course in global studies, Explorations I (mathematics), Applying Basic Skills in Mathematics, and an elective. All of these courses grant credits for high school graduation.

At Edison High School (one school with a New Beginnings program), I observed an excellent Haitian Creole and ESOL teacher, Ms. Basquias, who openly discussed with her students issues of adaptation to the United States. For example, she had students discuss and propose ways of handling aggression in the world outside the classroom. She combined traditional Haitian teaching practices (such as choral reading) with more open-ended, meaning-making activities and readers' theater. Familiar with the worlds of both immigrant and mainstream students, she had developed instructional strategies and materials that helped harmonize both worlds and that modeled for her students the ways in which they could combine different cultural practices.

Use of Traditional Documentation Procedures

American schools require papers that document the courses that students have taken. It is often impossible for immigrant students to obtain transcripts of their studies in their home countries, however, because of sudden departure from their homelands or bureaucratic barriers to obtaining documents in their countries. This is typical for immigrant students from the former Soviet Union and from war-torn countries. In some cases, the lack of documentation concerning prior schooling results in students having to take unnecessary classes. In others, if such documentation is required for school registration, immigrant teenagers may not be able to attend.

Another problem arises from the credits given for specific courses. For example, for students to meet the A–F requirements to apply to the University of California system, only 2 semesters of ESL can count as language arts credits. Immigrant students usually spend 6 or more semesters in ESL classes, which means that 4 or more semester courses do not count for college entrance. On the other hand, language arts classes in students' native languages—such as Tagalog for Tagalog speakers or Spanish for Spanish speakers—count either as foreign language courses or not at all. Because only 4 semesters of foreign language credit are required to enter the state University system, important time and effort spent in such courses is not acknowledged. It would make sense to count the first 2 years (instead of the first 2 semesters) of ESL as foreign language credit and to grant language arts credit for the native speaker classes, if the content, function, and spirit of such courses meets language arts standards.

Many schools offer sheltered content courses—also called Specially Designed Academic Instruction in English (SDAIE)[3] in California—to English language learners. These courses use special pedagogical strategies to teach the mainstream curriculum of a discipline. Teachers are supposed to select concepts that are both central to the subject matter and helpful to students in generating new understandings, but there is great variability in the quality of teaching and learning that takes place in sheltered classes (Olsen, 1997, p. 102). School officials face the dilemma of what to name a course (e.g., "World History" or "Sheltered World History") in students' academic transcripts. Both courses are supposed to cover the same material and develop the same understandings in students, but recording a course as sheltered in a transcript can jeopardize a student's college entrance options. Some universities do not count sheltered or SDAIE classes for admission. I have visited schools where the course, with no qualifier (e.g., "World History" instead of "SDAIE World History") is listed in the students' transcript along with a grade. This guarantees that the courses taken by English language learners will count for university admission. Some teachers argue that because these courses are watered down at their schools, the transcript should be a fair representation of what the students study. Where that is the case, however, concern should be directed to correcting the watering down of the offerings rather than accepting sheltered teaching as "dumbed-down" content.

---

3. Labels for different types of courses for English language learners have been in a state of flux in California. *Sheltered* (History, for example) and SDAIE (Specially Designed Academic Instruction in English) were used interchangeably for grade-level subject matter courses taught in English with special pedagogical designs for students learning English. Proposition 227 appropriated the term *sheltered* for English immersion courses—classes taught exclusively in English to beginning-level English language learners—which proposers of the measure called Sheltered English Immersion (SEI). As a result, in the current usage there is a big difference between sheltered and SDAIE classes.

Offering accelerated and academically rigorous summer academies for English language learners can help them develop their academic and sociolinguistic competence. If carefully planned and optimally taught, these academies can work especially well for underschooled adolescents. Unfortunately, summer offerings are often perceived as remedial. They are often planned poorly, lack appropriate pedagogical materials, and staffed with inexperienced teachers (the pay for summer school teaching is much lower than for regular academic year teaching). Summer programs often become control centers where everything but the exercise of discipline is watered down.

That this does not need to be the case can be illustrated by a personal anecdote. In the summer of 1988, I taught summer school in Salinas, California, for what I was told would be a small group of ESL students. I was excited about the possibility of trying my best with the same group of learners 4 hours a day for 8 weeks. I felt that the 50-minute periods that I had as a teacher during the regular academic year were unsatisfactory, and I dreamed of being able to work with the same group for 2 hours or more. To my surprise, I had 54 students in that summer class, I was offered no materials (because summer students could ruin the regular books that were to be used during the year), and on the first day of classes, I realized that my students were at all levels of English proficiency and literacy. Fortunately, I was offered a teacher aide who was fabulous. Although not knowledgeable about second language teaching, she was full of energy and ideas and motivated to learn. A graduate of one of the district schools, Carmen had distinguished herself and won a full scholarship to Harvard. She was a junior at the time, and every summer she had gone back to Salinas to be with her mother and to work. Having been an English language learner herself, she was eager to help others develop their potential. Carmen and I worked together countless hours preparing lessons and materials for different groups of students. At times we had students work together in small groups with others that had similar instructional needs, and at other times we combined them in more heterogeneous groups. We had a rewarding summer and developed a good friendship with each other.

This experience illustrates that summer academies can help English language learners make progress in their academic studies. It also shows that students once classified as Limited English Proficient can be used effectively to help teach these summer academies. They are in a position to act as positive role models, and their prior experiences can be channeled into effective work. Some of them may decide to become professional educators.

It is also important to note that not only do most English language learners come from disadvantaged socioeconomic backgrounds, but they also attend schools that are impacted by poverty. For example, between the late 1970s and the early- to mid-1990s, the poverty rate for young children in the United States increased by 30% among the White population, while it grew by 54% among Hispanics, who constitute the largest percentage of English language learners, and by 15% among Blacks (National Center for Children in Poverty, 1998). According to the 1990 U.S. census, 77% of English language learners in U.S. schools were eligible for reduced-price or free meals, compared with 38% overall in the same schools. Prospects, a congressionally mandated national longitudinal study of representative students in Chapter 1/Title 1 programs, found that a large percentage of English language learners attended schools where between 75% and 100% of their classmates live in poverty (August & Hakuta, 1997).

As we have seen, the very structure of American secondary schools can create serious barriers for immigrant students. Not only are the structures significantly different from those that students experience in their home countries, but also some practices, such as tracking, seem to work systematically and pervasively against their educational success. While programs such as AVID and New Beginnings have been able to counteract some of these problems, there need to be more programs like these to help immigrant students overcome the barriers of American secondary schools. We also need to seriously consider structural changes that would benefit *all* secondary school students, not just immigrants.

Effective Teaching and Learning Contexts for Immigrant Students

Effective teaching and learning for immigrant adolescents occurs in schools that promote the success of these students and of the student community as a whole. Lucas, Henze, and Donato (1990) conducted a study of six high schools in California and Arizona that were known for having good programs for their Latino English language learners in order to identify the features of these schools that promoted the success of these and other language minority students. The study identified the following key features:

- Value is placed on the students' languages and cultures.
- High expectations of language minority students are made concrete.
- School leaders make the education of language minority students a priority.
- Staff development is explicitly designed to help teachers and other staff serve language minority students more effectively.
- A variety of courses and programs for language minority students is offered.
- A counseling program gives special attention to language minority students.
- Parents of language minority students are encouraged to become involved in their children's education
- School staff members share a strong commitment to empowering language minority students through education.

Having identified the features that made these schools successful, the study provided concrete examples of how these features were realized in individual schools. Two years later, Lucas (1993) produced a checklist for schools to use to reflect on and discuss their level of commitment to the education of their language minority students and the extent to which these features are in place (see Table 3). In 1997, Lucas described ways in which schools can help immigrant students to move effectively through school and beyond school to further education and work. These three publications provide guiding principles for schools to create environments in which immigrant students can succeed.

Table 3. Checklist: Does your secondary school incorporate effective elements of schools for language minority (LM) students?

Effective Elements

A. THE SCHOOL CONTEXT

1. **Value is placed on the students' languages and cultures.**
   School staff:
(a) Learn about students' cultures.
(b) Learn students' languages.
(c) Hire bilingual staff with cultural backgrounds similar to those of the students.
(d) Encourage students to develop their primary language skills.
(e) Allow students to speak their primary languages.
(f) Offer advanced as well as lower division content courses in the students' primary languages.
(g) Institute extracurricular activities that will attract LM students.
(h) Other.

2. **The use and development of students' native languages are supported in a variety of ways.**
(a) Students use their native language to:
   (1) assist one another inside and outside class
   (2) tutor other students
   (3) write for class assignments
   (4) interact socially
   (5) other
(b) Teachers and instructional aides use students' native languages to:
   (1) check comprehension
   (2) explain activities
   (3) provide instruction
   (4) interact socially with students
   (5) other
(c) In the larger school context:
   (1) Administrators use students' native languages
   (2) Library books are provided in students' native languages
   (3) Parents receive communication in their native languages (e.g., letters, phone calls, forms to fill out)
   (4) Other

(Table 3 continues on the next page.)

Table 3 *(continued)*

3. **High expectations of language minority students are made concrete:**

   Schools:

   (a) Hire minority staff in leadership positions to act as role models.

   (b) Provide a special program to prepare LM students for college.

   (c) Offer advanced and honors bilingual/English language content classes.

   (d) Provide counseling assistance (in the primary language if necessary) to help students apply to college and fill out scholarship and grant forms.

   (e) Bring in representatives of colleges and minority graduates who are in college to talk to students.

   (f) Work with parents to gain their support for students going to college.

   (g) Recognize students for doing well.

   (h) Other.

4. **Staff development is explicitly designed to help teachers and other staff serve LM students more effectively.**

   Schools and school districts:

   (a) Offer incentives and compensation so that school staff will take advantage of available staff development programs.

   (b) Encourage all staff to participate in staff development focused on LM students.

   (c) Provide staff development for teachers and other staff in:

       (1) effective instructional approaches to teaching LM students

       (2) principles of second language acquisition

       (3) the cultural backgrounds and experiences of the students

       (4) the languages of the students

       (5) cross-cultural communication

   (d) Other.

5. **Families of LM students are encouraged to become involved in their children's schooling.**

   Schools provide and encourage:

   (a) Staff who can speak the parents' languages.

   (b) On-campus ESL classes for parents.

   (c) Monthly parent nights.

   (d) Parent involvement with counselors in the planning of their children's course schedules.

   (e) Neighborhood meetings with school staff and parents.

(Table 3 continues on the next page.)

Table 3 *(continued)*

(f) Early morning and/or late night meetings with school staff and parents.

(g) Telephone contacts to check on absent students.

(h) Potlucks.

(i) Other.

6. **Support services and extracurricular activities serve and include language minority students.**

These include:

(a) Peer tutoring.

(b) Teacher/staff mentoring.

(c) Career planning.

(d) College preparation activities.

(e) Multicultural awareness activities.

(f) International clubs.

(g) Cultural/ethnic groups.

(h) Sports teams.

(i) Other.

B. CURRICULUM

7. **The school's curriculum is designed to take into account the fact that language minority students are heterogeneous and have varied needs.**

It offers:

(a) Native language development classes (e.g., Spanish for Spanish speakers literature).

(b) ESL classes.

(c) Content classes in English.

(d) Content classes in students' native languages.

(e) More advanced content classes designed for LM students (e.g., calculus, government, physics).

(f) Less advanced content classes designed for LM students, as needed.

(g) AP and/or Honors classes for LM students.

(h) International clubs.

(i) Cultural/ethnic groups.

(j) Sports teams.

(k) Other.

(Table 3 continues on the next page.)

Table 3 *(continued)*

C. STAFF FEATURES

8. School leaders make the education of language minority students a priority.

They:

(a) Hire teachers who are bilingual and/or trained in methods for teaching LM students.

(b) Learn about the communities the school's students represent.

(c) Are knowledgeable of instructional and curricular approaches to teaching LM students and communicate this knowledge to staff.

(d) Take strong leadership role in strengthening curriculum and instruction for all students, including LM students.

(e) Are bilingual minority group members themselves.

(f) Advocate for LM students in the school and community.

(g) Other.

9. Administrators and other staff who are not formally part of special programs for LM students actively support such programs and services.

They:

(a) Promote and seek staff development focused on LM students.

(b) Include issues relevant to LM students on meeting agendas.

(c) Work with district bilingual/ESL staff.

(d) Attend activities sponsored by LM groups in the school and community.

(e) Speak up in favor of programs and services in various forums.

(f) Other.

10. All staff are knowledgeable of various aspects of education for LM students.

(a) Staff development on LM issues is provided and encouraged for mainstream as well as bilingual/ESL staff.

(b) Language development strategies are incorporated into content area courses across the curriculum.

(c) Staff in all role groups participate in staff development on LM issues (administrators, teachers, instructional aides, counselors, and others).

(d) Staff in all role groups, departments, and programs see the education of LM students as part of their responsibility.

(e) Other.

11. Counselors give special attention to LM students.

They:

(a) Speak the students' languages.

(b) Are of the same or similar cultural backgrounds.

(Table 3 continues on the next page.)

Table 3 *(continued)*

(c) Are informed about postsecondary educational opportunities for LM students.

(d) Believe in, emphasize, and monitor the academic success of LM students.

(e) Are available to the students who most need their services.

(f) Other.

12. **School staff members share a strong commitment to empowering language minority students through education.**

    They:

(a) Give extra time to work with LM students.

(b) Actively challenge the inequality of the social and political status quo.

(c) Reach out to students in ways that go beyond their job requirements, for example, by sponsoring extracurricular activities.

(d) Participate in community activities in which they act as advocates for LM students.

(e) Other.

13. **School staff members actively promote programs and services for LM students.**

    They:

(a) Attend school, district, and community meetings to provide information about LM students, programs, and services.

(b) Bring up LM student issues and needs in formal and informal discussions with colleagues.

(c) Seek opportunities to discuss LM student issues and needs with the local press.

(d) Highlight student successes in a variety of forums (at meetings, in newsletters, in newspapers).

(e) Actively seek collaboration with other district and community agencies to provide services to LM students.

(f) Sponsor cultural events for public attendance.

(g) Other.

D. **LONGEVITY & PERVASIVENESS OF EFFECTIVE FEATURES**

14. **The elements of effective schooling for LM students are present throughout the time they are in the secondary school.**

15. **The elements of effective schooling for LM students are present across all of the educational experiences of LM students in the secondary school.**

Note. Adapted from *Applying Elements of Effective Secondary Schooling for Language Minority Students: A Tool for Reflection and Stimulus to Change* (Program Information Guide No. 14, pp. 15-24), by Tamara Lucas, 1993, Washington, DC: National Clearinghouse for Bilingual Education. Used with permission from NCBE. A full version is available without cost from NCBE.

In their 1990 study, Lucas, Henze, and Donato focused on macro-features of secondary schools—the institutional structures needed to promote the success of Latino students who are learning English—an important starting point when looking for promising programs for immigrant students.

During my visit to the programs selected for this study, I wanted to look inside classrooms to observe and analyze how instruction for English language learners was being orchestrated, how this instruction engaged the students, and what teachers and students had to say. For this purpose, I observed and audiotaped classes, took notes, and interviewed teachers, students, and parents to get a fuller picture of the impact that pedagogical arrangements can have on English language learners' schooling. I was guided by current theories of teaching and learning that hold that learning requires the active construction of mental models by the learner and that "when new information or ideas are encountered, the individual must think about and figure out how they fit within the existing structure or must reorganize their mental schema to accommodate the new knowledge" (McLaughlin & Shepard, 1995, p. 9).

From this process I derived a set of 10 priorities to help teachers evaluate and improve the quality of instruction in their classrooms. Although some teachers in this country do apply these priorities when designing and delivering instruction in classes that have English language learners, they have not always reflected on what these priorities are, nor have they systematized them as constituting the base that undergirds their pedagogical approach. Because instruction remains frustrating for many students, not just for those learning English and content simultaneously, it is appropriate to highlight these priorities. Furthermore, we seldom ask those most affected by teaching and learning for their suggestions. Students' voices are typically absent from discussions of the quality of their schooling, yet students have valid information that can guide our critiques and plans. Thus, I included the voices of immigrant students (quotes taken from my interviews) to develop the priorities and guide the discussion here.

How each teacher articulates and implements these priorities greatly depends on the teacher's own characteristics, the characteristics of the students, local circumstances, and other relevant aspects of the context. There is no single approach applicable to every student or in every teaching situation, no "one size [that] fits all" (Reyes, 1992). Varied approaches and methods are needed, depending on the local context.

Ten Priorities to Consider When Designing Instruction for Immigrant Students

1. The culture of the classroom fosters the development of a community of learners, and all students are part of that community.

High school is hard for me because my English is so limited. Sometimes it is hard for me to do things because of my English. There are times when I feel a lot of pressure because I want to say something, but I don't know how to say it. There are many times when the teacher is asking questions, I know the answer, but I'm afraid that people might laugh at me. I know I just need to be a little patient with myself.

(10th-grade student from Mexico, 2 years in the United States)

To me, the big issue is that we need more teachers who care about us, who treat us as human beings, who greet us and want to help us. Too many teachers don't really care. They are just doing their job, coming to school and going home.

(9th-grade student from the Philippines, 3 years in the United States)

In effective classrooms, teachers and students engage in the co-construction of a culture that values the strengths of each person and respects their interests, abilities, languages, and dialects. Within these classrooms all participants in the class, including the teacher, move among the roles of expert, researcher, learner, and teacher, supporting themselves and others. Immigrant teenagers bring a variety of experiences to the classroom that, if correctly tapped, can serve as a springboard to new explorations that can enrich everyone's experience. As Bialystok and Hakuta (1994) have noted, "the exciting challenge for teachers and learners of a second language is to construct a context for creative and meaningful discourse by taking full advantage of the rich personal, cultural, and linguistic backgrounds of the participants" (p. 203).

The two quotes above from students illustrate what happens when this culture does not exist; students feel insecure, ashamed, and unwelcome. The establishment of a respectful, nourishing, and challenging culture with high expectations for everyone is a *sine qua non* for the success of English learners. Also necessary is the understanding that in a classroom with a warm, accepting climate, it is not embarrassing to admit one's limitations. As Jesús in Ferreiro, Pellicer, Rodríguez, Silva, & Vernon (1991) admitted, as he volunteered to continue the read-aloud in class: "Yo leo, es que yo no sé leer bien ... para enseñarme" ("I read ... I do not know how to read well ... so that I can teach myself) (p. 8). Jesús understood that in his class it is acceptable to confess one's inability to read well. He also knows (i.e., he has been taught) that one learns to read by reading. If Jesús wanted the opportunity to practice, he deserved to have that opportunity. The other students in the classroom were attentive and patient, even though Jesús's reading was not very clear because they understood that their attention would help him become a better reader.

While expectations for all learners are high, it is also understood that students will not progress at the same pace or in the same ways but will move differentially toward the attainment of goals, as we will see exemplified in the program profiles in chapter 5.

2. Good language teaching involves conceptual and academic development.

I am sick and tired of what we do in our ESL class. We are always going shopping to the supermarket, as if all we did in life was eat ... I need to get ready for the other classes. I am lost in World History, for example. Why can't we study something like this in ESL?

(16-year-old from El Salvador)

When I entered the regular English classes, I found they were much more difficult than the ESL classes. It made me feel that I didn't walk, but jumped from the ESL to regular classes. I had to study very hard to recover the gap. I wish schools can have a better ESL program so the transition is easier. (mainstreamed student from Vietnam)

Effective ESL classes, even at beginning levels, can focus on themes and develop skills that are relevant for teenagers and for their studies in mainstream academic classes. Students are not helped if what they do is trivialized or presented to them atomistically. In contrast, discussing similarities and differences in families around the world, even in the first week of class, can help students develop vocabulary that will prove useful in other classes later on, such as "structure," "nuclear," "extended," "role," "responsibility," and so on. Likewise, if the teacher presents a mini-lecture and shows students how to take notes—for example, by helping them draw the family tree of a student she just described—they can learn academic skills (such as note taking) that can be transferred to other contexts. Immigrant students need to learn not only new content, but also the subject-specific ways of discussing it, the language and discourse associated with the discipline. Therefore, all subject matter classes must have a language focus as well.

Effective teaching prepares students for high-quality academic work by focusing their attention on key processes and ideas and engaging them in interactive tasks in which they can practice using these processes and concepts. ESL teachers need to know what linguistic and cognitive demands they are preparing their students for and plan to help them develop the necessary linguistic, cognitive, and academic proficiencies. Content area teachers need to determine what knowledge in their field is crucial and what is not. It is not uncommon to hear secondary school teachers say they teach a specific point because the program calls for it or because it is the next point in the curriculum. Because of an overreliance on curricula and textbooks, teachers are sometimes more focused on getting through them by the end of the semester or year, or on not skipping some part of them, than they are on what students are learning or need to learn (see, e.g., Ball & Rundquist, 1993).

3. Students' experiential background is used as a point of departure and an anchor in the exploration of new ideas.

What I don't like about this class is that the teacher thinks we were born yesterday, that we do not know anything of value. It is true I do not know a lot, but back at home I was a good student, and I was always informed about what happened in the world. The other day the teacher was talking about the U.N. and asked if anybody knew who the Secretary General is. I responded Pérez de Cuellar, and she gave me such a funny look, as if I had said something bad. Then, after a second, she said the same name with such a pronunciation that you would have never recognized it.

(18-year-old from Colombia, 2 years in the United States)

Why was I sent to the office? There is this new girl in class, and I was helping her because she does not understand a thing that goes on. I thought I did not, either, but when Carmen asked me for help I realized I did, and I was explaining to her in Spanish, and the teacher got mad. She said, "Don't you know I do not understand Spanish?" And I answered, "So? Carmen needs help." But I got a referral.

(15-year-old from Mexico, 28 months in the United States)

Immigrant adolescents know a great deal about the world, and this knowledge can provide the basis for understanding new concepts in a new language. However, the knowledge they already have is often overlooked because of the misconception that students who have studied elsewhere or have not had previous formal schooling are *tabulae rasae* on which knowledge needs to be imprinted. The tendency to see immigrant students as blank slates derives in part from their minority status: Because they hold a subordinated and less prestigious position in society, they are not perceived as possessing valuable knowledge. Another reason that teachers do not tap into students' prior knowledge during instruction is the traditional transmission model of teaching, which assumes that it is the teacher's role to pass on important knowledge to students, who lack it.

Students will learn new concepts and language only when these are firmly built on previous knowledge and understandings. Tharp and

Gallimore define comprehension as involving "the weaving of new information into existing mental structures" (1988, p. 108). As students realize that their everyday knowledge is not only valued in class, but is also desired, a sense of trust and competence is achieved that promotes further development. This does not come easily at first. Some students have been socialized into lecture and recitation approaches to teaching, and they expect teachers' monologues to tell them what lessons are about. However, after engaging in activities that involve predicting, inferring based on prior knowledge, and supporting conclusions with evidence, they will realize that they can learn actively and that working in this way is fun and stimulating.

If understanding involves weaving new information into pre-existing structures of meaning, then teachers must help English learners see connections through a variety of activities. In preparation for a mini-lecture, for example, a teacher may present an advance organizer such as a fishbone map (see Figure 2) and walk students through the most important information that will be discussed. (Other well-known graphic organizers include Venn diagrams, compare/contrast matrixes, cause/effect circles, anticipatory charts, story graphs, and open mind diagrams; see, e.g., Adger et al., 1995; Crandall, Jaramillo, Olsen, & Peyton, in press). Before students are asked to read a passage in their world history textbook, for example, the teacher tells them that the passage will explain four main reasons for the First World War. As she draws the organizer on the board

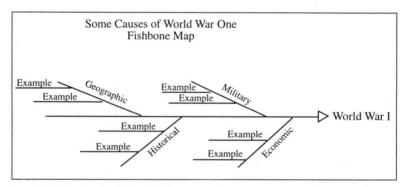

Figure 2. A fishbone map used to prepare immigrant students to read a difficult social studies text in English

and asks students to copy it for their use in taking notes, she foreshadows the content of the reading and provides specific examples of each category of reasons.

The use of advance organizers serves several purposes: It promotes schema building before a topic is introduced; it focuses learners' attention on important aspects of the information to come; and if the diagram is used for note-taking purposes, it alleviates students' anguish by letting them know beforehand what information they should be able to understand and take notes on. Students in general, and English learners in particular, need to be able to process information from the top down—to have general knowledge of the broad picture before studying the details—as well as from the bottom up—vocabulary, syntax, and rhetorical devices to understand the language. Furthermore, by viewing the skeleton of a passage in advance, students' apprehension is lowered, helping them tolerate ambiguity and encouraging them to be willing and accurate guessers. Rubin (1975) has argued that these are some of the most important qualities of a good language learner.

The effective teaching of second language learners also involves Vygotsky's concept that "the only 'good' learning is that which is in advance of development" (1978). The Zone of Proximal Development (ZPD) is the area of potential growth the learner may enter if given the right kind of guidance. In this process, social interaction is essential. Jerome Bruner (1986) extends this notion with the concept of interactional scaffolding, instruction that enables students to take risks safely and extend their abilities with the help of their teachers and more capable peers. Scaffolds are used as support mechanisms to allow English learners to handle tasks involving language that is too complex for them to understand or produce. Without such support, students might not succeed. Scaffolds are temporary; that is, as the teacher observes that students are capable of understanding and producing language on their own, she gradually hands over responsibility to them. "Kidwatching," to use Yetta Goodman's apt expression (1978), implies that the teacher carefully monitors each learner's growing understanding and developing academic skills, providing scaffolds and challenges as the need arises. Rather than simplified tasks or language, English language learners require amplification and enrichment of the linguistic and extra-linguistic context. With this type of instruction they do not have just one opportunity to come to terms with the concepts to be learned, but instead may construct their understanding on the basis of multiple clues and perspectives encountered in a variety of class activities.

One strength that adolescent teenagers bring to this country is age-appropriate communicative competence in their own languages. This knowledge can be helpful at times for the negotiation of classroom concepts that may be inaccessible otherwise. Let us imagine, for example, a student from Russia who has lived in the United States for several years and has consequently developed the ability to understand most of what goes on in his science class. A recently arrived student from Russia has joined his class. Occasional interactions in Russian between these two students can be beneficial for the newcomer when his efforts to make sense of concepts and processes in English are met with failure. If the teacher treats these interactions in Russian as productive, while at the same time scaffolding her instruction for the new student enough so that he can—besides using his native language—also participate in English tasks, she will be validating the importance of the student's prior knowledge and enhancing his opportunities to construct new understandings in a supportive climate.

At times, as the above-quoted student from Mexico revealed, a teacher may become suspicious of students having brief interactions in class in a language the teacher cannot understand and may interpret these interactions as rebellious behavior. Understanding that students scaffold for each other through these exchanges in their native language can help teachers to put similar incidents in perspective. The incident illustrates how helping the newcomer helped the more experienced student to realize that she understands more about the subject than she would have given herself credit for.

4. Teaching and learning focus on substantive ideas that are organized cyclically.

I used to get very upset because I couldn't understand everything the teacher said. I just stopped listening. But Ms. Long always gives us the main points before she explains or we read, and then a few days later she touches on the same topics but with different materials. Now I know if I am patient, I can understand everything that is important.

(10th grader from Brazil, 2-1/2 years in the United States)

I love the themes in our ESL book because you read about the same problems in many different stories, and you understand them better every time. I think all classes should be in themes. (student from Poland, in the 2nd year in an American school)

Working effectively with English learners requires that teachers select from the many themes that comprise a subject area those that are central to the discipline. Schwab (1964) calls these themes *substantive* and connects them to the *syntactic* structures of a field, which include the canons of evidence and proof that are shared by subject matter communities. These key concepts form the basis of the curriculum taught. They should not be organized in a linear progression of items, but rather the curriculum should be based on the cyclical reintroduction of concepts at progressively higher levels of complexity and interrelatedness. Cyclical organization of subject matter leads to a natural growth in the understanding of ideas and to gradual correction of misunderstandings. The concern for immediate comprehension, an assumption of linear curricula, negates what we know about learning. As Howard Gardner (1989), speaking of education in general, says,

First of all, when you are trying to present new materials, you cannot expect them to be grasped immediately. (If they are, in fact, the understanding had probably been present all along.) One must approach the issues in many different ways over a significant period of time if there is to be any hope of assimilation. (pp. 158-159)

As we develop the academic skills of immigrant students, we also need to inform them about this cyclical aspect of the learning process to help ease their frustration over not mastering new content and skills immediately. Furthermore, if teachers carefully choose the key concepts to be explored in class, these will serve to generate future understandings as students progress in their schooling and in English.

5. New ideas and tasks are contextualized.

I couldn't make any sense of what happened in the middle ages and the lives people led. I could understand "castle" and imagined a beautiful castle in my dreams. When the teacher showed us a 4-minute clip of an old film, it all clicked, and I could make sense of all those other words—knights and vassals and all of that.

(8th-grade student from Ethiopia, 3 years in the United States)

In my chemistry class I can always do well because the teacher first demonstrates an experiment, and then we try a similar one. Then he asks us to write down the procedure and the conclusions in groups of two or four. I can do it. I can even use the new words because I know what they mean.

(10th-grade student from Chile, 3 years in the United States)

English language learners often have problems in classes trying to make sense of decontextualized language. This situation is especially acute in the reading of textbooks. Secondary school textbooks are usually linear, dry, and dense, with few illustrations. Embedding the language of textbooks in a meaningful context by using manipulatives, pictures, a few minutes of a film, and other types of realia can make language input comprehensible for students. It is sometimes assumed that contextualization consists of using pictures to help convey ideas, but any sensory environment that is created to illuminate new information helps to contextualize new language and concepts. Teachers may provide verbal contextualizations by creating analogies based on students' experiences. This, of course, requires that the teacher find out about students' backgrounds because a metaphor or analogy that may work well with English speakers may not clarify meanings for English language learners. In this sense, good teachers of immigrant students continually search for metaphors and analogies that bring complex ideas closer to the students' world experience. With the increasing availability of CD-ROM, the Internet, and other new technologies in schools, it is essential that teachers of immigrant students learn to use them. They are especially suitable for use with immigrant students because the teacher can select and sequence material for particular groups of students that provides a rich textual, visual, and auditory basis for understanding.

6. Academic strategies, sociocultural expectations, and academic norms are taught explicitly.

In Korea there is a class which teaches Korean customs and traditions, like what you do and eat at a funeral. It is all throughout junior high and high school. Students are taken to a separate building where elders teach the class. It is very serious. I wish they had something like that here in the United States, so I could learn the customs and how to be an American.

(middle school student from Korea, 2-1/2 years in the United States)[4]

What I really love about my ESL teacher is that she explains to us how to organize our thoughts and how to write in school ways. She also teaches us what to do to be good, critical readers. That is so helpful in my other classes, and I know it will be good for life.

(10th-grade student from Mexico, 2 years in the United States)

Effective teachers develop students' sense of autonomy through the explicit teaching of strategies, or plans of attack, that enable them to approach academic tasks successfully. The teaching of such metacognitive strategies is a way of scaffolding instruction; the goal is to hand over responsibility to the learner and automatize the necessary skills. In reading, for example, instruction in strategies such as Reciprocal Teaching can be very successful in helping students construct their understandings of English texts. In Reciprocal Teaching (Brown & Palincsar, 1985; Palincsar, David, & Brown, 1992), a teacher and a group of students take turns leading a dialogue aimed at revealing the meaning of a text. During this dialogue, the assigned teacher (an adult or a student) summarizes the content, asks questions concerning the gist of the reading, clarifies misunderstandings, and predicts future content, all of which involve comprehension-fostering and monitor-

---

4. I am indebted to Laurie Olsen for this student's quote.

ing strategies. Teachers need to judge if their English learners are ready to engage in reciprocal teaching and scaffold the activity as needed. For example, initial practice in reciprocal teaching may focus on how to summarize a text and ask good questions. From then on, other components can be added.

In addition, Delpit (1995) argues that the discourse of power—the language used in this country to establish and maintain social control—should be taught explicitly to minority students, since it is not automatically acquired. Guidance and modeling can go a long way toward promoting awareness of and facility with this discourse. For example, preferred and accepted ways of talking, writing, presenting, and so on are culture specific. In an exploratory study of the written discourse of several languages, Kaplan (1988) discovered that the way in which Americans structure their discourse follows a linear, deductive progression in which each paragraph is structured in the "this is what I am going to say—I am saying it now—this is what I said" format. While British written discourse is also structured linearly, it is inductive, thus giving rise to some British criticism that American writing is boring. Latin writers, on the other hand, and Spanish writers in particular, can proceed through many zigzags in which the topic shifts into parallel explorations and then goes back to the main idea. Unless a Spanish-speaking writer is explicitly shown these differences in writing styles, he may tend to apply the structures preferred in his native language to English, thus producing writing that appears chaotic to North American teachers and students. However, explicit teaching of the rules of the discourse of schooling is only a first step in the scaffolding of students' performance. In a second stage, students need to become ethnographers, collaboratively studying the reality of this culture and discerning its rules, so they become proficient participants in it.

Student awareness of differences, modeling by teachers of preferred situated behaviors, and study by students themselves of differences and preferred behaviors are three steps in the development of learner proficiency and autonomy that need to be included in the education of language minority students to make them effective in their multiple worlds.

7. Tasks are relevant, meaningful, engaging, and varied.

If you want me to be honest, the biggest problem here is that we're BORED! We spend too much time sitting in classes that are dead, unexciting. Teachers talk to the blackboard, and always lecture, lecture, lecture. It's the same day after day, every day, every period, except when they get mad because somebody complains or does something to wake us up. It's boring. You can't just sit through that. And sometimes it really is too much, and that's when you think, Why should I get up to go to school? What am I getting out of it?

(9th-grade student from Mexico, 3 years in the United States)

Classes would be more interesting if teachers themselves were excited, had us do interesting things, and related subjects to what is happening around us. I hate it when all we do is silly worksheets. Why can't we work on projects? There is this teacher in school that everybody loves because he always has students doing things, presenting them, and teaching each other. He even included a chapter on Mexican history that my friends in that class loved. Why can't more teachers be like him? If more were that way, I am sure more students would stay in school and learn.

(10th-grade student from Mexico, 2-1/2 years in American schools)

Most classes for immigrant students are monotonous, teacher-fronted, and directed to the whole class; teacher monologues are the rule (Ramírez & Merino, 1990). If students do not interact with each other, they are not given opportunities to construct their own understandings, so naturally they often become disengaged. Because immigrant students are usually well behaved in class, teachers are not always aware that they are bored and are not learning. Good classes for immigrant students not only provide them with access to important ideas and skills, but also engage them in their own constructive development of understandings.

It should be mandatory for every teacher of immigrant students to shadow a student for a day at school and to get first-hand knowledge of their usually passive schooling experience. Most teachers, having experienced school from the students' perspective, would most likely want to transform their teaching.

8. Complex and flexible forms of collaboration maximize learners' opportunities to interact while making sense of language and content.

I learned so much from the World Religions project. At first, I thought it would not be so interesting because I am not especially religious. But as we started our research, and then exchanged information and viewpoints, I could see there were so many similarities among such different religions. It is the same way we feel here, we come from many nations and many languages, we all look different on the surface, but underneath we are very similar and share a lot. That is why we like to collaborate. It helps us see all those important things.

(high school student from Russia, 3 years in the United States)

I always think that it is better for me to work in small groups because then I am not afraid to participate. I am basically a very shy person, and if I have to speak in front of everybody, I rather die. In small groups nobody is afraid, not even to make a mistake.

(middle school student from Cambodia, 4 years in the United States)

Collaboration is essential for second language learners because in order to develop language, they need opportunities to use it in meaningful, purposeful, and enticing interactions (Kagan & McGroarty, 1993). In the best classes I have observed, rather than having individual students present to the whole class, teachers use the jigsaw configuration: They regroup the students who have worked collaboratively on various projects into new formations to present to other small groups what they have learned. In this way, all students' oral presentations convey new information to a small group. The group may later use this information for other activities such as discussing a problem and solving it jointly, and then writing about it individually.

Collaborative work needs to provide every student with substantial and equitable opportunities to participate in open exchange and elaborated discussions. It must move beyond simplistic conceptions that assign superficial roles to second language learners, such as being the "go getter" or the "time keeper" for the group (Adger et al., 1995). In these collaborative groups, the teacher is no longer the authority figure. Students work autonomously, taking responsibility for their own learning.

The teacher provides a task that invites and requires each student's participation and then hands over to the students the responsibility for solving the problem. While teachers supply the tasks, they do not provide learners with specific questions to be answered, but rather encourage them to take a personal perspective on the topics that arise in small-group discussion.

Collaborative tasks do not involve learners in routine procedures, but instead present them with problems that have complex solutions, with no single right answer or standard set of steps (Cohen, 1994). These tasks should move toward maximal student involvement, in which they choose the theme they will investigate and the focus and strategies for their investigation.

9. Students are given multiple opportunities to extend their understandings and apply their knowledge.

One of my favorite activities is to do Open Mind diagrams. Trying to present what is going on in the mind of Kino at this moment of *The Pearl*, for example, helped me clarify my ideas. I could use quotes, phrases of my own that synthesize the main ideas, drawings, and symbols to do it. Cool! I have memorized the teacher's instructions! Working on Kino's mind, I realized that a person can feel two very contrary things at the same time. By the time I had to write, I was ready for it, and I didn't do so bad.

(8th-grade student from Guatemala, 4 years in the United States)

The United Nations simulation? I loved it! After we read so many different perspectives on the Palestinian situation we can see many different sides, and in the U.N. discussion we can discuss and try to win new understandings. It is difficult to imagine an easy solution to the problem. (10th-grade student from Romania)

One of the goals of learning is to be able to apply acquired knowledge to novel situations. For English learners, these applications reinforce the development of new language, concepts, and academic skills as students actively draw connections between pieces of knowledge and their contexts. Understanding a topic of study involves being able to perform in a variety of cognitively demanding ways (Perkins, 1993).

In one of the schools I visited, the teacher of an ESL class gave students opportunities to do this. After the class had read a myth using a variety of interactive tasks, the teacher divided the myth into three sections. Groups of students were assigned to write the dialogs that they thought might have occurred during a particular moment of the myth. Although these dialogs were developed collaboratively within each group, each student kept his or her own script and used it for the final performance of a drama on that section. Students analyzed, compared, made connections, hypothesized, monitored their understandings, assisted each other, and finally transferred the knowledge they acquired to a new situation, re-presenting a narrative text as a dramatic one. This teacher's approach did not primarily depend on transmitting knowledge, but rather on scaffolding her instruction so that her students could perform in complex ways. Learning to explore cause and effect, examining the main components of a myth, and looking for evidence to support an interpretation were all developed and refined over time. The teacher's main purpose was to develop her students' ability to use English in a variety of school contexts beyond her class, which she did by structuring her lessons so that substantive concepts, and the language needed to express them, could be developed. (See also Olsen & Jaramillo, in press, for another example of such teachers.)

10. Authentic assessment is an integral part of teaching and learning.

When we first started keeping a collection of our writing, I thought that was a dumb idea, but now I see some value in it. The other day, I was reading one of my compositions from January and I asked myself "What? What did I say here? I don't get it." The teacher had told us this would be good for us because it will show us how to improve, and how we improve. I guess he was right. I can now see I write a little bit better in English. I thought I had not moved.

(8th-grade student from El Salvador, 2-1/2 years in the United States)

Boy, was I nervous the day before the presentation of my senior project. I wished I was in ESL II so I could do it in Spanish, but then, talking to my friends who were doing their presentation in Spanish, they were just as nervous as me. So we decided to rehearse together one more time. I felt good because the rehearsal made me realize that I understood the topic of my research better than anybody else, and that I could probably answer the questions from the jury. How did it go? Fine, I was nervous at first, but when I started presenting and I looked at my panel and they were smiling, I forgot about my nerves and continued. The whole thing went by fast and well.

(12th-grade student from Mexico, 3 years in the United States)

Assessment should be done not only by teachers, but also by learners, who assess themselves and each other. Considerable research supports the importance of self-monitoring in the learning of second languages (O'Malley & Chamot, 1989; Oxford, 1990; Rubin & Thompson, 1982). Authentic assessment activities engage second language learners in self-directed learning, in the construction of knowledge through disciplined inquiry, and in the analysis of the problems they encounter.

For example, correction of pronunciation errors is especially effective when students are put in charge of monitoring their own oral production in English. This can be done by recording, within each collaborative team of students, the individual presentations at the final stage of a jigsaw project. The cassette recordings can then be given to students to listen to their own presentation and to write comments reflecting on it—analyzing their production, pinpointing troublesome areas, and exploring corrective strategies.

Likewise, portfolios of student work can powerfully indicate to students their progress in the acquisition of English and academic dexterity, as the first student quote above indicates. This is especially important during the intermediate stages of language development, when students tend to feel that they are not progressing very much. Other experiential assessment practices, such as self-evaluation narratives, the use of rubrics, and the senior project, also hold promise for the education of high school immigrant students. Some of these practices are described in the program profiles in chapter 5.

Authentic assessment is embedded in everyday practice: How is a given student performing? At what stage is she in the development of her ability to express a sequence of events? Is she ready to take the lead in a reciprocal teaching activity? All of these questions, which teachers ask themselves every minute of their teaching, are assessment activities, and they inform and determine teaching arrangements. All good assessment, then, provides learners with opportunities to learn and helps teachers determine what and how to teach.

A Model for Teachers' Understandings

If English language learners are to have access to challenging, rigorous, and relevant curriculum, we also need to consider what teachers need to know about themselves, their students, the milieu in which they operate, and the overall role of schooling in students' development. Given the complexities of immigrant students' lives, the nature of American secondary schools, and the societal and cultural context in which schooling takes place, teaching immigrant students effectively is not merely a matter of technical expertise. An accomplished teacher possesses a broad range of understandings and abilities that guide important decisions and specific actions from minute to minute in the classroom.

What is the knowledge base that informs all of these decisions and actions? I will use an adapted version of Shulman's structural model of teacher understanding (Shulman, 1995; see also Walqui, 1997), designed with classes of native English speakers in mind, to discuss the different areas of knowledge that accomplished teachers possess. This model presents five elements of teachers' knowledge, including their vision, understanding, practice, motivation, and reflection.

Vision

This category encompasses teachers' ideologies, objectives, and dreams, all of which provide a sense of direction to their students' learning. What are a particular teacher's goals for the future of society? What are the roles that she or he sees immigrant students occupying in that society? Does this teacher see language as having ideological implications? Does this teacher believe in the value of bilingualism? Is this teacher satisfied or dissatisfied with the status quo as it relates to immigrant students? Does this teacher believe in the power of students to construct a better society for everybody?

Understandings

This category represents the range of cognitive understandings that inform instruction: general pedagogical knowledge, subject matter knowledge, and pedagogical content knowledge.

• **General pedagogical knowledge** comprises the corpus of knowledge and skills concerning learning, learners, and the goals and processes of education. General principles of instruction, such as the importance of collaboration, wait time, and the development of metacognitive skills belong in this area.

• **Subject matter** knowledge is teachers' knowledge of what Schwab (1964) calls the substantive and syntactic structures of the subject area. The substantive structures include main concepts in the field and the paradigms that give structure to the subject and guide future developments. The syntactic structures of a field include the canons of evidence and proof that are shared by subject matter communities. In the case of ESL or sheltered content courses for English language learners, subject matter knowledge includes awareness of the role and power of language in cognition, learning, and social life in addition to knowledge about the English language as a system of communication (Darder, 1991; Fairclough, 1989, 1993; van Lier, 1995).

• **Pedagogical content knowledge** is the knowledge that teachers possess about how to teach a specific subject, and themes within that subject, to groups of students. It includes access to multiple forms of representation for concepts, including the use of appropriate examples, metaphors, similes, and ways of structuring the teaching of a specific point to make it accessible. This weaving of new concepts together with ways of presenting them to second language learners is what makes the teaching of immigrant students especially complex. Pedagogical content knowledge also encompasses an understanding of how English as a second language is best acquired by immigrant teenagers and how to embed content in the tea•hing of the language.

Practice

This category represents teachers' skills and strategies for transforming their goals and understandings into practice. Understanding alone is not enough without the ability to act on it in effective ways. In fact, at times teachers can articulate a coherent grasp of what *ought* to be happening in a class, but there is a discrepancy between their knowledge and their ability to implement it.

Motivation

Motivation derives from the reasons, incentives, and emotions that give energy and meaning to a teacher's visions, understandings, and practice. Given the current anti-immigrant climate in this country and the difficulties that school systems have meeting the needs of immigrant students, this component is crucial for teacher effectiveness because without it, good teaching is not possible.

Reflection

A good teacher has the capacity to revisit past teaching experiences, or the experiences of others, with the purpose of learning from them to become more effective in the future. Through reflection on practice, teachers decide what to incorporate into their permanent repertoire and what to refine or discard, thus actively contributing to their continuous retooling as teachers.

These elements of teacher knowledge are dynamic: They interact with and enrich each other. They also operate in the context of a teaching community that encourages learning and growth. It is important to examine all of these components of teacher knowledge to assess whether a teacher can work well with English language learners. A given professional, for example, may be very knowledgeable about his subject matter and about educational theory, and when teaching mainstream students he may know exactly which anecdotes to tell to make a point in a presentation to his class. But if he does not understand that anecdotes rely on culturally shared knowledge and culture-specific humor and uses only U.S.- or English-based anecdotes, his presentations will be ineffective with the immigrant students in the class. This is one of the ways in which generally effective teaching differs from effective teaching for second language learners. Teachers of second language learners need to be attentive to the crucial forms and functions of language, so that they do not unduly burden students with all of the information available. In this way, they shape their instructional practices to address their students' needs and abilities.

Promising Programs and Practices for Immigrant Students

In this chapter, I profile four programs that are working to address the needs of their secondary school immigrant students. To select these schools, I solicited nominations from knowledgeable people with national, state, and local responsibilities and followed up on recommended sites and individuals with telephone interviews. Four sites were then selected for week-long visits, during which I observed classes and interviewed students, teachers, parents, and other relevant personnel at length. I also collected written documentation, took notes, and audiotaped the classes I visited. I later selectively transcribed the audiotapes for the classroom vignettes included here. In general, numerical data that would allow examination of student outcomes was not available, primarily because it is customary not to give English learners the standardized tests required of most students because most of these tests are in English. In California and many other states, however, English language learners now have to take tests along with their English-speaking counterparts.

Three of the schools are in two of the states with the largest populations of immigrant students—California and New York. I was also interested in exploring the issues faced by schools in other states that are experiencing increased immigrant enrollment, but not at the same levels as are California, Florida, Illinois, New Jersey, New York, and Texas (Espenshade, 1997), so I selected a program in Iowa. Whether large or small, districts with schools that have had an influx of even small numbers of immigrant students are faced with numerous issues similar to those faced by schools with large immigrant populations.

The programs chosen are at different stages in the development of their services for English language learners and continue to improve what they have in place. They exemplify different programmatic approaches, from a Newcomer Center approach in Sioux City, Iowa, to a high school especially designed to offer optimal learning environments for immigrant students and their teachers, as is the case with International High School in Long Island, New York. These programs also exemplify both the challenges and the possibilities of educating English learners. My objective is to review the promising practices as well as the limitations that are typically faced by middle and high schools around the country. I hope these cases can help further discussions across the country about how to educate immigrant students in secondary school. At the end of each program profile, contact information and materials available from the program are listed.

The Reception Center, Sioux City, Iowa— A Focus on Comprehensive Services

The staff of the Reception Center in Sioux City, Iowa, are continuously improving the quality and efficiency of the services they provide to the growing immigrant population. Places like Sioux City are often included in discussions of the challenges of educating immigrant students because the percentage of immigrant students and English learners is relatively small. In the last decade, however, the growth rate of the English language learner population in Sioux City has exceeded the rate of growth in many other highly impacted places. Because this situation is relatively new, teachers, administrators, and other school staff were not prepared for it. They also tended to believe that these students were the exclusive responsibility of the ESL teachers. This belief absolved the other teachers of the need to retool themselves to meet changing societal needs and work with new groups of students. These are some of the issues that the Sioux City program struggles with as it works to provide immigrant students with solid opportunities to enter mainstream education and life in the community.

The Setting

Sioux City lies on the Missouri River in northwestern Iowa, at the Iowa–Nebraska–South Dakota border. It is part of the Greater Sioux Cities, which also encompass South Sioux City, Nebraska, and North Sioux City, South Dakota. With a population of 80,505 (1990 census), the city is the commercial center for the surrounding agricultural area. Tractors, trucks, machine products, fertilizers, and feed have traditionally been produced in the area. In the last few years, new and active meat-packing and computer industries have helped the city reduce its unemployment rate to 2%. For example, North Sioux City is home to Gateway 2000, the largest mail order computer company in the world. The jobs generated by these activities attract immigrants, who move to Iowa from other parts of the country where jobs are scarce.

Sioux City is a clean, quiet, and organized community where extreme weather is the norm. In winter the temperature can drop as to low as –25º with a wind-chill factor of –85º, while on the hottest summer days, the temperature rises into the hundreds with very high humidity. Natives of the area love outdoor activities and celebrations when the weather permits, and they are proud of the beautiful recreation areas afforded by the confluence of three rivers—the Missouri, the Big Sioux, and the Floyd. Hunting for deer, duck, goose, pheasant, and coyote is popular, and the area's rivers and lakes are noted for their stock of catfish, northern pike, and bass. Annual festivals include the Siouxland Multicultural Ethnic Fair, a week-long event in the spring season, and the Rivercade Festival in July.

The city became the center of national attention on July 19, 1989, when United Airlines Flight 232 exploded in a fireball and crash-landed in one of its corn fields. The efficient and rapid response of the local people, who had been warned of the airplane's attempt to land at the local airport, helped save the lives of more than half of the passengers. Sioux City citizens were prepared for the emergency because the whole community regularly practices disaster training and drills.

Previously a center of Indochinese resettlement, more recently Sioux City has received Mexican and Central American laborers and their families, both documented and undocumented. When the first wave of immigrant Indochinese students arrived in Sioux City, there were no teachers prepared to work with them. In 1978, the Sioux City Schools started a centralized orientation program at one school with one teacher and a few Vietnamese students. The number of immigrant students in the district remained small until the 1988-89 school year. Since then, the school population of English language learners has more than

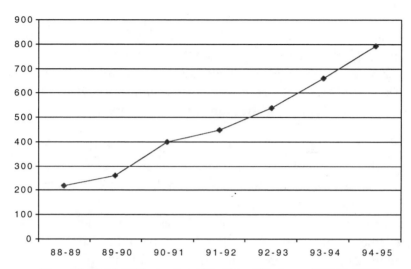

Figure 3. District ESL enrollment in Sioux City, Iowa, 1988 to 1995

tripled (see Figure 3). Sioux City currently has Iowa's highest growth rate in numbers of immigrant students. I received an indication of the growing need to focus on educating second language learners when I visited the Reception Center in April of 1995. At that time, 145 students had already been registered in the ESL program for the next academic year, indicating both the increasing need for the Center and the hard work of Center personnel to keep in contact with immigrant populations in their community

At the secondary school level, the number of English learners grew from 48 to 261 students in the same time period. Although these numbers are not comparable to the immigrant populations in the major immigrant settlement centers in the country, the sudden increase nevertheless taxed the school system in ways for which they were initially unprepared.

About the Reception Center

How does a community traditionally characterized by linguistic homogeneity cope with linguistic diversity? Typically, midwestern schools have responded to immigrant students by placing them in their neighborhood schools, assigning them to grades in accordance with their ages, scheduling them in regular classes, and pulling them out for ESL instruction whenever feasible. An ESL teacher would travel from school to school to work with the few English language learners for periods of 20 to 60 minutes daily, depending on the need. As the number of students needing this help increased, the ESL pull-out sessions became shorter and less frequent, and the demands placed on the itinerant ESL teacher became increasingly harder to meet in a sensible way.

In response to this unsatisfactory situation, the Sioux City Community Schools Reception Center was established. Recognizing that they had a limited number of teachers prepared to work with English language learners, district staff decided to concentrate those teachers in one building. There students could spend half of the school day learning English and subject matter through specialized ESL instruction that prepared them to work in sheltered content and mainstream classes the rest of the day. Since immigrant students have needs in addition to academic instruction, the Reception Center also connects them with other available services.

Intake and Exit Procedures

Whenever new students arrive in Sioux City, they go to the Reception Center, located in downtown Sioux City in school buildings known as the Central Campus, for individual assessment and placement. Center director Caroline Donaway and the home–school liaison person greet the newcomers and begin developing profiles on them. Students are tested in English, if they have some knowledge of the language, or in their native language (Spanish or Vietnamese at the time of my visit) by teacher aides who speak their languages well. These teacher aides have been working for the local schools for many years and are consequently aware of the academic and social demands that will be placed on the students when they enter the regular program.

The Reception Center has tests in Spanish and Vietnamese, supplemented by a reading test and a writing sample, which are kept in the students' files. Students are placed in the ESL program if they score at level 4 or lower on the English proficiency test and do not read at or near grade level on the Gates-MacGinitie reading test. Students are tested yearly, and when they reach level 5 and can read close to grade level, a decision is made about whether to exit them from the ESL program. The director, an ESL teacher, the principal, and a classroom teacher hold a conference to decide whether the student should continue receiving ESL instruction, receive tutorial assistance, or exit. All students continue to be monitored after they exit. If necessary, they can re-enter the ESL program after exiting. In addition, students can exit the program in stages; if they receive both ESL reading and ESL speaking instruction, they can exit one class one year and the other class the next. They can continue to receive tutoring in content area classes from an ESL tutor after they have exited, if the classroom teacher requests it.

Every decision about a student's program is made in teams at the Center. Ms. Donaway and her staff discuss the new arrivals, the courses they have been assigned to, and the mainstream teachers who will receive them. They also discuss the progress that students are making and contact the teachers at the receiving schools to find out how students are doing and how Center staff can support them while they are there.

While at the Center, students take ESL classes and work on reading and writing in English. Since there is a good wood and metal workshop at Central Campus, one period every other day is scheduled for the students to work there, if they choose. During my visit to the program, I observed students producing furniture that was going to be used in a new computer laboratory that the Center was planning to open for the 1995-96 academic year. I could see the students were very happy while working in the workshop. One of them told me, "This is a great way to learn English because the teacher shows you what the meanings of the words are, so we all understand and learn at the same time."

Reception Center Staff

To meet the educational needs of its immigrant population, the state of Iowa has instituted programs that prepare teachers to become certified in the teaching of ESL. Although the number of these teachers is increasing, there are still not enough to teach all of the students enrolled in the schools in the state. In addition, certified teachers tend to concentrate in the larger urban areas of the state, which is why the Reception Center was established. The Center now has 30 staff members and more than 700 students. Of these students, 65% speak Spanish, 24% speak Vietnamese, 3% are Laotian, and 3% are Cambodian.

Program director Caroline Donaway is an experienced ESL teacher who is fully bilingual in Spanish and English. She has lived in the community for over 30 years, working in the schools for much of that time. She knows the community very well and has many connections there, which has made it easier to establish support mechanisms outside of school for the students in the program. When she first started teaching in the district, Ms. Donaway taught Spanish as a foreign language. Since she had lived and studied abroad, she seemed to be the logical person to be in charge of teaching the new immigrant students at one of the schools in 1978. When the number of students needing ESL instruction began to grow, and it was no longer possible for her to teach all of them, she approached the teachers whom she knew would be caring and supportive of second language learners and would enjoy the challenge of working with them.

Since the Center was established, ESL and sheltered content teachers have been carefully selected by Center and school district staff to work at the Center and the receiving schools. Ms. Donaway and the home–school liaisons provide these teachers with information about their students' backgrounds so they can engage them in class. This personal, careful process in the selection and support of teachers instructing immigrant students has remained a feature of the Reception Center that extends to all of the schools that receive them. Ms. Mehringer, a science teacher in one of the receiving schools, is one of those teachers.

She told me, "I love teaching the ESL students. They are so serious and always attentive. They also work very hard. I can see how much they progress by the ways they participate in my classes."

Ms. Donaway said the following about the types of teachers the Center selects.

Not everybody can work well with our students. It usually helps if people have studied another language and lived in a country where a language other than English is spoken. This gives them the basis to understand the frustration students feel when they cannot adequately express their ideas, when a lot of what is going on is not comprehensible or semi-clear. These teachers are also more willing to try different ways of teaching their subject matter, and in the end, they discover that these techniques can also be good for mainstream kids.

Program Culture

The work of Center personnel is based on the strong conviction that given appropriate support, immigrant students will succeed in their new lives in the United States. They have a clear vision of what English learners can achieve and of how they can contribute to American society. Center staff feel that the presence of a culturally and linguistically diverse student population enriches their schools. Much care has been taken to create a climate of support and encouragement for students and teachers in the Center and in the sheltered and mainstream classes that the English language learners attend.

In spite of an expressed commitment in the district to support diverse student populations, Center staff are aware that once students are out of their program, they are likely to face discrimination. Consequently, they engage students in open discussions of what to do if they face discriminatory situations and other difficulties when they are away from the security of the Center. The teachers find that this explicit preparation is necessary and have confirmed this belief through conversations with students who have exited from the Center. Mr. Gould, the district's Equity Director, also talks with the students about situations they may encounter, including possible harassment, and explains the appropriate avenues for dealing with such incidents.

Another important aspect of this program is its work with social service agencies to support students outside of school when necessary. Connections are made with the Sioux Land Refugee and Immigration Network, local adult ESL programs (to inform parents about ESL classes), preschool services, The Stork's Nest, Head Start, community colleges, and other community service organizations.

The creation of La Casa Latina, a support agency designed to work with Spanish-speaking families, is an excellent example of how proactive Center personnel have been in supporting the needs of their students and families. The first immigrant students, primarily Vietnamese and Cambodian, were sponsored by social service agencies (such as the Iowa Bureau of Refugee Services and Lutheran Social Services), which supported families and helped them become oriented to their new environment. Having a heated place to live, for example, was absolutely critical if families arrived in the winter, but few families arrived with enough money to pay a housing deposit and advance rent. The sponsoring agencies helped families address these issues and collected used winter clothing and furniture from the community for them.

Because the Latino immigrants are not part of a structured resettlement process, they do not have connections to sponsors like these, so Ms. Donaway and other concerned members of the community wrote a proposal to create La Casa Latina. This agency offers information in Spanish about health services; helps Latino families with translation, interpretation, and counseling; and provides them with an initial loan. La Casa Latina has started an after-school program for students who are at risk of dropping out of school, offering them a safe place to meet, study, play, and get academic support. The program is staffed by La Casa Latina employees working in conjunction with volunteers from the community. Many of the volunteers are students who have exited from the ESL program, and some of them study at the local community college.

English as a Second Language Classes

The purpose of the beginning and intermediate ESL classes is to develop conversational and academic competencies in English. These classes meet for 4 periods daily for the entire academic year. The materials used are selected from commercially produced textbooks, general interest books with many pictures, and materials designed by the teachers working in teams. Although the classes focus initially on survival language, they also include explicit teaching of skills connected to reading, writing, listening, and speaking in a new language.

For students who have just arrived, these classes start with an orientation to the community. Students work with maps of the city, finding the schools they will be attending, the school bus routes, and other landmarks. These maps are used to introduce and practice key vocabulary and expressions related to finding the way to school. Then the students are taken on the bus to become familiar with their daily routes and to experience what they practiced in the classroom. The same procedure is followed by the ESL teachers in the receiving schools, to familiarize the students with their new environments and reduce the possibility of their getting lost in large schools. This is only one example of the types of activities that students engage in to help them feel comfortable in their new environment. Other activities include preparation for the severe winter weather, such as learning how to listen to the news for announcements that school will be starting late or be canceled.

Subject Matter Classes in Students' Primary Languages

Recognizing that recently arrived adolescents need to continue their academic development as they learn English, the Center offers them a few subject area classes in Spanish and Vietnamese. These are taught by American teachers who speak Spanish proficiently and by native Vietnamese teachers. The Spanish for Spanish speakers and Vietnamese for Vietnamese speakers classes are based on the premise that language is not only important socially, but that it is also an important tool for cognitive development. The skills and conceptual understandings constructed in the native language will be available for use in the English language after the student has acquired a threshold level of English proficiency.

Sheltered and Mainstream Content Classes

Transportation is provided for students to move from the Reception Center to their receiving schools. During their first year of studies, students take sheltered science and math classes taught exclusively for English language learners at the receiving school. These classes present selected coverage of the topics addressed in equivalent mainstream classes and grant credits toward graduation. The materials used in the sheltered science classes are selected from available textbooks that include more pictures and diagrams than do most textbooks to facilitate students' comprehension. The careful selection of key themes from the curriculum enables teachers of sheltered classes to spend more time covering less material than is covered in the mainstream classes. In the second year, students still attending the Center are placed in sheltered social studies classes that grant credit and in selected mainstream classes taught in English. They usually also fulfill the required second-year requirements in art and physical education.

Instructional Practices

Many characteristics of the primary language, ESL, and sheltered content classes make the program in Sioux City one that nourishes and challenges immigrant students, regardless of differences in their backgrounds. Ms. Donaway and her staff at the Reception Center have created a respect for diversity, a belief that immigrant students can succeed in American schools although it may take them longer, and an acknowledgment of the students' diverse strengths. The teachers I observed worked carefully to prepare their students for readings, involved them in many interactive activities, and provided useful scaffolds so they could stretch their abilities in a safe, supportive environment. To give a more in-depth portrait of how these classes worked, I profile three of the classes I observed below.

A content-based ESL class

One of the intermediate ESL classes that I visited at the Reception Center was preparing to read the story of Arachne, a Greek myth about a proud weaver who defies the goddess Minerva and as punishment is turned into a spider. As class started, the teacher asked the students to fill out an anticipatory chart (a graphic organizer with two sections, one to note what the student knows about a topic and the other to list a few questions the student has about the topic). The teacher drew the diagram on an overhead transparency, and the students copied it into their binders. The title read: *Arachne: A New Myth.* Under this were two section headings that read (1) *This is what I already know* and (2) *I want to find out.* The teacher then gave the students a few minutes to make some notes in their individual charts. The teacher told me this was the fourth myth they were reading in class, and I knew that the students enjoyed this text and the task because they were all actively writing on their charts. One student wrote in the first section, "It gives an explanation" and "Something fantastic is going to happen." Another wrote, "a very old story, has a lesson"; in the second section, he wrote the question, "Who is Arachne? Any connections to Arachnophobia?"

Next, students worked in pairs, talked about their answers, and wrote in their charts the parts of their partner's response they did not have. While students were engaged in their sharing of ideas, the teacher walked around the room, listening attentively to several groups. She then handed the students the reading, which had been photocopied, and asked them to take 2 minutes to flip through the pages, after which, in agreement with their partners, they added a few more ideas to their charts. The reading was six pages long and had three large pictures. The teacher then asked the class to share their ideas in pairs about what the story might be about. At this point, students noticed the names Arachne and Minerva in the text and connected them to the pictures. The two students sitting next to me added three questions to the second section of their charts: "What does the goddess Minerva do in the story? Is Arachne the name of another goddess? What does the big spider do?" Having built on their prior knowledge about myths to anticipate possible ideas about the reading, and after using contextual clues to further anticipate developments, the students were ready to start reading.

The teacher then asked students to copy from the overhead projector a compare/contrast matrix comparing Arachne's and Minerva's personal characteristics, activities, and feelings. This graphic organizer signaled to students the key information they would need to understand from the reading. It also structured for them important aspects of the story, which they understood was about two characters whose very different personalities resulted in consequences to be discovered at the end of the story. The teacher read the first paragraph of the myth aloud and asked the class if there was any information from it that could go into the compare/contrast matrix. Students now knew that Arachne was a young woman who was an excellent weaver and that Minerva, the goddess of intelligence, was also a very good weaver. After several other ideas were discussed and written, she asked students to read the next two paragraphs in silence and write the relevant information in their charts. She told them she would have a whole-class discussion in 5 minutes.

I have just described about 15 minutes of a very animated and participatory ESL class. The rest of the session proceeded in similar fashion, combining individual work in anticipation of dyadic interaction with the use of varied graphic organizers to help students focus on the most important information in a text that contained numerous expressions beyond the students' ability to comprehend. The students were not deterred by the complexity of the language; they knew they could trust the teacher to point them in the right direction.

Tapping into students' prior knowledge was central at the beginning of this lesson; then the emphasis shifted to understanding the ideas presented in the text by connecting and comparing information. The teacher had used these techniques with her students previously and reminded them that the strategies used in class could be used in their other classes as well, with modifications. The students seemed to appreciate this type of teaching. Cristina, a Mexican student, told me that she learned a lot of English from the readings done in class and, probably more important, that she had learned how to be a good reader. She said, "The teacher told us in the past that good readers review their knowledge of a subject before they read. In class, that can be done with webs of ideas, anticipatory charts, or just brainstorming, but in real life it is enough to stop for a minute and think after you read the title of a story or a book."

A sheltered science class

One of the sheltered science classes I observed at North High School focused that day on human reproduction. The class met in a laboratory filled with plants, full bookshelves, bone collections, and models. For this particular class, plastic models of the male and female reproductive systems were used to identify organs, trace trajectories, and talk about functions. That afternoon there were 16 teenagers in class, 10 boys and 6 girls, a balanced mix of Vietnamese and Latino students. I was impressed by the seriousness with which the students asked each other questions and explained processes. The teacher distributed photocopied diagrams from the book so the students could take notes on their individual copies. She then modeled a question-and-answer process, pointing to plastic models in front of the class and using the overhead projector to write key phrases that pairs of students could use for practice in naming the reproductive organs and their functions. She encouraged them to point to their diagrams as they asked questions of each other. A section of a transcript from that class reads as follows:

(Vietnamese boy): What is the name of the canal that leads from the uterus to outside the body?

(Mexican boy): Vagina. And what is the name of the muscular organ in which the fetus develops?

(Vietnamese boy): Uterus. What is the name of the organ where fertilization takes place?

This exercise took about 5 animated minutes. Whenever a pair of students did not have the answer, they would turn around to ask another dyad if they knew it. The teacher's rule in this class was "ask three before you ask me," a rule that many students I interviewed seemed to enjoy.

After another task in which, working in pairs again, students were invited to write down two or three questions they would like to investigate, the teacher asked the students to read in their books. Five minutes were devoted to skimming through the text individually, after which the teacher conducted a whole-class oral reading with discussion. At the end of the class, the teacher foreshadowed what would be covered in the next class (the 9-month process of gestation) and assigned homework. The book used in this class was the regular life science book used in mainstream courses, and English learners taking this course received science credit.

This class, which uses hands-on activities to contextualize new concepts and language, allows students to cover important topics in the science curriculum while developing their ability to use high school scientific discourse. Students were constantly engaged in the construction of their understandings through interaction with peers and the teacher in English. They were eager to participate in the exchanges proposed by the teacher and did so with seriousness. While I was observing, I could imagine the smiles and hesitation that the same conversations would engender in a mainstream class.

A Spanish class for native Spanish speakers

The Spanish class I observed at the Reception Center similarly engaged students in critical discussions and tasks. This course attempts to cover the primary concepts included in mainstream English language arts classes. On that day, students were reading "The Scholarship Jacket," a story by Marta about a Chicana's triumph over discrimination in a Texas middle school. The issues brought up in the story were relevant to the students and triggered animated discussions. Here, too, the students were working with graphic organizers as they read the story and were asked to predict what would happen next at key moments. This work was conducted in groups of four. Students were asked to consider what they would have done if they had been in the protagonist's situation. Martín, one of the students profiled in chapter 1, was in this class. Although it took him a bit longer than other students to write and take notes, when it was time for discussion and raising questions, he was quick and thoughtful with his contributions.

The Spanish for Native Speakers curriculum fosters Spanish-speaking students' development of speaking, reading, writing, and critical thinking skills in their native language with the understanding that these skills can be transferred to English. Students do not need to lag behind academically while they develop enough English proficiency to read sophisticated literature in English. This goal is being met in Sioux City because there are materials to teach classes in Spanish and teachers prepared to teach them. The Latino students I interviewed felt very happy to read Latin American and Spanish literature that raised issues and realities that they felt close to, as well as American and English literature in Spanish translation. This opportunity helped them understand their new reality and also prepared them for their eventual experience in mainstream literature classes. Similar opportunities are offered to Vietnamese students at the Reception Center.

Conclusion

The Sioux City Community Schools Reception Center has multiple strengths, the most vital one being the staff's respect for immigrant students and belief in their ability to succeed educationally. There is a clear sense that the culture and language of the students is valued. Center staff also have a flexible approach to their ESL courses, rearranging schedules as needed based on students' progress. Student who advance rapidly are promoted to higher level classes and monitored supportively. The Center also promotes flexible time arrangements and is willing to extend the age limit for high school completion to help their immigrant students graduate. In Iowa, students can stay in high school until they are 21 years old. There have been several cases in which 21-year-old English language learners who needed an additional year to graduate from high school were allowed to stay and complete their studies. If students prefer, however, they are helped to make the transition into an adult program that will grant them a high school equivalency diploma.

In addition to the classes and resources provided during school hours, individual students can get help at the end of the school day. On occasion, mainstreamed students can also go to the Center for academic support after school. Connections with parents are also part of the support. If a student is absent, a call or visit is made to the home, and parents are kept informed at all times of educational arrangements and other important issues.

Center staff provide a great deal of support for their students and their students' families. Parent meetings are immensely successful because they are conducted in the families' native languages and because they respond to the concerns of the immigrant community. The week prior to my visit, for example, there had been a severe snow storm in the area, and because of the extreme temperature and road conditions, classes had been canceled on Monday. A parent meeting in Spanish had been scheduled for Tuesday evening. Center personnel expected just a few parents to show up and were pleasantly surprised when more than 100 people crowded into the Center, making local newspaper headlines. The success of this meeting demonstrates that parents indeed feel valued and supported. They want to stay informed about school affairs and to know how they can contribute to their children's academic success.

Staff at the Center work collaboratively, which is another one of their strengths. They discuss problems, review relevant literature together, and refine features of the program. This work is part of the teachers' professional growth, since as they engage in curriculum writing and discussions of students' work, they learn more about how their own work can improve in the future. They have developed an impressive array of thematic units to help make their everyday teaching more constructivist, engaging, and successful.

Of course, there are ways in which Center staff would like to improve the education of their immigrant students and grow as a program. They would like all teachers, including those at the mainstream schools, to believe that all students, including immigrant ones, are their responsibility. Many of the mainstream teachers feel that Center personnel should have primary responsibility for the smooth transition of immigrant students into the mainstream. Although Center personnel agree that they are better prepared than anybody else to educate English learners and promote their success in regular schools, they also feel that everyone in the district needs to share this responsibility. An increase in awareness and commitment at the receiving schools concerning the needs of immigrant students would greatly benefit the Center's students as they make the transition to those schools.

The Center would also like to expand the professional development of mainstream teachers in the district. Through the Multifunctional Resource Center in Madison, Wisconsin, which has an office in Minneapolis, Reception Center personnel are able to attend professional growth sessions on collaborative learning, the development of critical thinking skills in sheltered content classes, and so on. Although these services are announced to all teachers, usually only Center personnel attend and benefit from the sessions. Getting all teachers to recognize that they can learn from these sessions is a goal for the future.

Separating immigrant students for part of the day works to their advantage in many ways, but it can also contribute to negative perceptions of them in their regular schools. Some teachers, other students, and their parents think, "They are not as capable as other students, they need special services," or they ask, "Why do we have to teach them?" These negative perceptions can affect teacher expectations of English learners. If teachers have not had professional development to help them understand and work with these students, they feel disengaged from their education.

Materials Available

- Gates-MacGinitie tests in Spanish and Vietnamese
- Reading test and writing sample guidelines in Spanish and Vietnamese
- A curriculum based on thematic units for content-based ESL classes

Contact

Caroline Donaway
1121 Jackson Street
Sioux City IA 51105
Phone (712) 279-6079
Fax (712) 279-6747
E-mail donawac@sioux-city.k12.ia.us

Calexico High School, Calexico, California— A Focus on School Restructuring

Calexico High School, situated in a largely Spanish-English bilingual area, illustrates how committed teachers and administrators can restructure a school so it serves the educational needs of its English language learners. While once this high school left these learners to fend for themselves, it now offers challenging academic coursework in a supportive environment for all of its students. Despite the difficulties of such a radical change, Calexico High School has risen to the challenge, becoming an excellent example of effective education for secondary school English language learners.

The Setting

The community of Calexico lies on the southern border of the United States, a 2-hour drive through the desert east of San Diego, in the Imperial Valley of California. With 30,000 inhabitants, Calexico feels like a U.S. suburb of Mexicali, the Mexican city it shares the border with, which has a population of over a million. Calexico is a bilingual/bicultural community. Signs in Spanish and English advertise businesses and products. In the streets, offices, stores, and restaurants, one is as likely to hear Spanish as English spoken. There is also a clear perception that the relationship between Latinos and Anglos in the community is one of equality, a perception reinforced by the presence of a high-status Mexican American population occupying professional and managerial jobs in town.

Agriculture and livestock are the valley's major industries—in 1903 the Colorado River was diverted to provide water to the area, and in 1941 the All-American Canal created the Imperial Valley, where crops can be planted and harvested throughout the year. In 1991, commerce began expanding to accommodate a growing retail trade from both Mexican and U.S. patrons—large department stores and warehouses were built and became the town's main sources of employment (Neumann, 1996).

While there is a strong sense of equality between the Latino and Anglo populations in Calexico that is unmatched in the rest of the state, it is also true that there are few jobs and the pay is low. There is an extremely high level of unemployment (in 1992 Imperial County led the nation with a 30% unemployment rate), poverty (the average household income is less than $12,000 a year), and a serious drug abuse and drug trafficking problem (Calexico has one of the highest intravenous drug use rates in the nation).

These kinds of statistics are typically associated with high dropout rates from school, low academic performance, and low teacher morale. The Calexico educational system, however, has been bright and promising, with elementary and middle schools that have been models for the state for over a decade. The district consists of six elementary schools (Grades K through 6), two middle schools (Grades 6 through 9), one comprehensive high school, and one continuation high school. With 6,856 students—of whom 98% are Latino, 80% are English language learners, 30% are migrant students, and 51% receive free and reduced-price lunch—the dropout rate in the district is well below the 28% state average for Latinos. In 1990, 14.5% of the students dropped out of school; in 1992, 20.2% dropped out. Among the many recognitions that Calexico schools have received are three CABE (California Association of Bilingual Education) Exceptional School Awards, one National Chapter I Recognition Award, a Golden Bell Award, an R.J.R. Nabisco Next Century School Award, two restructuring planning grants for elementary schools, and two high school restructuring implementation grants.

Calexico High School

Calexico High School, located in the northeastern side of town away from the sounds of the downtown area, is a collection of spread-out, one-story buildings surrounded by green grass. The spaciousness is needed in Calexico, where the temperatures are extremely high all year. The school takes care of its own gardens, which help soften the impact of the weather. Students and adults alike warmly greet visitors.

When the school was originally built, no one expected the student population to grow as much as it did. As the school became unable to accommodate new students, portable classrooms were added. The excessive number of portable classrooms led the district to decide in 1993 to transfer the 9th graders to a new middle school that had just been built, so now the high school houses exclusively 10th through 12th graders.

During the 1994-95 academic year, the total number of students enrolled at Calexico High School was 1,541, of which 65% were learning English as a second language, nearly all of them Spanish speakers. Beginning in 1992, Calexico High School began restructuring, aided by an SB1247 California state grant, which provided funds for 5 years to implement a plan devised during the 1991-92 academic year. As a result of these efforts, the school is moving from a system characterized by tracking and an exclusive emphasis on the teaching of English as a second language to immigrant students, to a system that promotes high expectations, challenging teaching, and success for all students.

School Culture

Although once an unsupportive environment for English learners, Calexico High School now shares with the other schools in the district a district-level philosophy that guides their programs and the relationships among teachers, students, parents, school staff, and other members of the community. This philosophy is stated in the following principles:

- respect for students' culture, language, and background;
- a strong belief that all students can learn;
- equal access for all students to learn and pursue further education if desired;
- encouragement of parental involvement as a necessary component of education;
- a belief that schools should adapt to the needs of students; and
- encouragement, at the district level, of innovation, risk taking, and team building to achieve its goals.

(Calexico Unified School District, 1995)

These district principles translate into the norms, values, beliefs, and practices at Calexico High School described below.

Bilingual personnel

Sixty percent of the teachers at Calexico High School and all clerks and office personnel who provide services to students are bilingual in English and Spanish. One is as likely to hear Spanish as English used for personal and academic interactions, and teachers and other adults communicate as comfortably in English as in Spanish. Furthermore, most of the teachers in the school live in Calexico and feel they are important members of the community, sharing in its culture and values.

Course offerings in Spanish

Another clear signal that the students' native language is valued is that all academic subjects are offered in Spanish for students who are beginning their development of English as a second language. These courses are not watered-down versions of their English counterparts, but rigorous courses with curricula and materials that are aligned with the English courses and that grant academic credits for graduation. For example, the Spanish for Native Speakers class grants students Language Arts credits.

Belief in bilingualism as an asset for the future

Teachers at Calexico High School are convinced that bilingualism and biculturalism will prove advantageous to their students' future, as it has in their own lives. There are expectations in the community that with the North American Free Trade Agreement, the region may develop jobs, and that most of these jobs will require high skills, including bilingualism.

Educational materials in Spanish

Students have access to textbooks, literature books, technology, and other resources and services in their primary language. The school has invested a great deal of money, time, and effort into translating high-quality materials into Spanish.

Home–school communication

All notices are sent home in English and Spanish, and parent meetings are conducted bilingually.

High expectations

Personnel at the school share a strong belief that all students can learn. They hold high expectations for all students and clearly communicate these expectations to the community. Mechanisms are in place so that these expectations can be met.

Intake and Exit Procedures

Three criteria are used by the school to assess their new immigrant students' proficiency in English and determine their program of studies. The Secondary Level English Proficiency test (SLEP), which tests listening and reading comprehension, is used for placement into English as a second language classes (ESL I, II, or III). In addition, newcomers are interviewed by a teacher knowledgeable in the area of second language development to determine oral fluency in English. Finally, a writing sample in Spanish or English, which is scored holistically following criteria developed collaboratively by a group of teachers at the school, is required of all incoming students. The array of information about each student helps school staff to place students in the right combination of classes and to determine whether they need individualized support. Most of the incoming students perform close to grade level in reading, writing, and math. Although their proficiency in English may be limited or nonexistent, their command of Spanish and of basic academic skills, acquired in schools in Mexicali, Mexico, is usually adequate.

New immigrants are placed in a grade based on their grade in the school they last attended or on their chronological age, if there is a large discrepancy between their chronological age and the grade last attended. They are then assigned to the same academic programs as the other students in their grade, with two exceptions: (1) The choice of the language of instruction for subject matter classes is based on their command of English, and (2) if their English proficiency needs development, they are enrolled in English as a second language classes. Regardless of the language of instruction, all of the subject matter classes grant the same amount of credit toward graduation.

The Staff

As at most schools, the teaching staff at Calexico High vary in their level of preparedness to teach English language learners. Many possess a CLAD (California Cross-Cultural, Language and Academic Development) certificate offered by the California Commission on Teacher Credentialing. This credential indicates that they either have graduated from a university program that offers a CLAD emphasis or have completed a professional growth series on teaching English language development and content instruction to English learners and passed a test that measures their knowledge in this area. CLAD teachers, then, are essentially specialists in teaching English language learners.

Many teachers attended Calexico High School themselves and learned English as a second language (in 1995, 13 of the 75 teachers, or 17%). These teachers have a first-hand understanding of the challenges faced by immigrant students and the importance of acquiring solid content knowledge and skills while developing full English proficiency. There is a big difference, however, between the time when these teachers studied at the school and today. Many years ago, the school had a "sink or swim" philosophy in which all subject matter courses were taught in English, and it was the exclusive responsibility of the students to succeed in those courses. Many failed because engagement in academic activities in a language that one does not command is quite difficult. But this unfortunate experience has since motivated these teachers to restructure the school so that all of the students will have the opportunity to participate meaningfully and actively in their education.

In addition, in the past, very few students were encouraged to further their education after graduation from high school. Today, teachers who went through that system of low expectations, inefficient delivery of instruction, and low student performance are the ones committed to transforming the school into a system that will serve all students. One social studies teacher made the following comment:

As a student ... here, I kept on thinking, "Just because I do not speak English, I am not dumb." I would say to myself, "Why can't I become a professional in the future? Why do teachers assume we will all work in the fields? Why do we always do the same old simplistic stuff? Why do they think we are not capable? Where is this going to lead us? If I were the teacher, I would try to make my students dream of a better future, I would move fast in my teaching, and I would push them so that they achieve...." That frustration inspired me to become a teacher in order to break the vicious circle.

Professional Development

School restructuring has given teachers at Calexico High the opportunity to place the academic needs of all students at the center of their concerns. To plan for restructuring, teachers met regularly in disciplinary teams for 2 years to discuss their goals for their students. The first year it was difficult for them to engage in these conversations because they felt they were just repeating conversations they had had before. They requested professional development sessions on reaching consensus and found the sessions to be beneficial. After 2 years of goal setting, curriculum development, and implementation of the senior project (discussed below), many teachers felt they needed to concentrate on instructional strategies. Some teachers, supported by the school, participated in summer institutes run by the University of California's Subject Matter Projects to learn to assist students in the development of their academic and linguistic skills. Because these sessions are typically held in the summer and in San Diego, a 2-hour drive away, not all teachers are available or willing to attend. Those who have attended these institutes, which include sessions on literature, writing, math, social studies, science, and the arts, have found that the experience has triggered many changes in their teaching.

Instructional Practices Shaped by Restructuring

Restructuring at Calexico High School introduced a number of essential changes designed to benefit all students, particularly those learning English. These included the creation of academies and institutes, detracking, comparable curricula for native English speakers and English learners with bilingual materials, and a senior project.

Academies and institutes

In the 10th grade, students are organized into academies—arrangements of 150 students assigned to a specific team of teachers. There are currently four academies at the school, one of which is an ESL academy. This clustering helps students feel connected academically, socially, and emotionally to other students and adults and follows the California Department of Education's recommendations for improving secondary schools (as expressed in *Second to None: A Vision of the New California High School*, 1992). Another advantage of this type of organization is that it allows professional collaboration among teachers, enabling them to plan integrated units of teaching, share strategies, exchange information about students, prevent incipient failure, and contribute to increased achievement.

School staff are also planning to establish institutes for the 11th and 12th grades that will offer in-depth, specialized concentration in an area of study that emphasizes applied academics and leads to postsecondary education or work opportunities. They plan to offer certificates of competence for students who attend the four institutes developed by groups of teachers: Business and Economics, Visual and Performing Arts, Human Services and Engineering, and Technology.

When I visited Calexico High School, I observed a planning session for the Human Services and Engineering institute. Five teachers were working to generate themes that would be appropriate for multidisciplinary treatment. Much of the discussion focused on the importance of clarifying the objectives, with teachers deliberating about whether the topics and texts they had selected were relevant for the students and whether talking about a specific process would help students understand, apply, and evaluate other processes. Teachers also discussed expected student performance outcomes both during the unit and at its culmination. Once teachers knew what they wanted their students to achieve, they could develop specific tasks to achieve those goals. They could also think of other topics and texts that would be appropriate in order to enrich instruction for students who were in the process of developing English and help them establish links across the disciplines.

As the five teachers shared ideas, I could see a community in action, with members clarifying for each other essential components of their beliefs and their dreams. Every time an idea was discussed, one more step was made toward the achievement of consensus. This is the kind of working community that many committed teachers dream of participating in. It is also an efficient way to foster professional growth.

Detracking

As a central element of restructuring, Calexico High School teachers decided to do away with the school's tracking system. This decision was possible because the school decided to offer three options for all required courses—Spanish, English, and sheltered English—and to grant the same number of credits for all of them. All courses were to provide academic challenges for students that would open doors to post-secondary education and other opportunities. The teachers based this decision on the knowledge that previous arrangements had not worked for the students and on a review of research in the field. Emily Palacio, the district Assistant Superintendent of Instructional Services, explained the decision as follows:

While we believe that the acquisition of English is of the utmost importance, we realize that second language fluency is a long process and that we must continuously support and nurture language development. However, experience and research have taught us that the development of cognitive skills will have a much greater impact overall on long-range academic outcomes. Thus, our primary goal is to develop academic proficiency, regardless of language.

Consequently, Calexico High did away with basic courses and began teaching demanding courses for all students. The Mathematics department, for example, adopted the College Preparatory Math (CPM) program, which moves from pre-algebra in the ninth grade to math analysis and calculus in the upper grades.

An immediate benefit of doing away with basic courses was that teachers' discussions could focus on essential questions of quality, coverage, appropriate level, and instructional delivery that would guide all the courses. As Gil Méndez, a teacher leader in the restructuring movement at the school, told me,

Instead of discussing whether a class is to be offered in English or Spanish, our dialogues now center on the issues of how courses are going to address everybody's needs, how we are going to include everybody, what it is that we want all of our students to achieve, and more constructive concerns in general.

Comparable curricula and bilingual materials

Demanding academic courses in students' primary languages require curricula and materials to support the delivery of challenging content. For the College Preparatory Math I and II courses, for example, Calexico staff chose to use CPM materials, which emphasize that students co-construct mathematical understandings through hands-on experimentation, inquiry learning, and collaboration. Because the program was originally developed in English, the district spent $9,000 to have it translated into Spanish so that all classes would work on the same concepts, at the same level, and through the same pedagogical arrangements. District staff considered the expense an indispensable step toward offering all students access to the same high-quality education and guaranteeing equal access to the same mathematical content. In the words of the Assistant Superintendent of the district, "If we wait until someone does it for us, we are saying that our English-as-a-second-language students can wait while the others move forward. It is a matter of, do you want to provide equal access or don't you?" ("School Expects," 1993). Today, English, sheltered, and Spanish math classes are comparable in content, expectations, form of delivery, and academic credits. A similar process is being implemented in other curricular areas.

In the three versions of the language arts curriculum, the same themes and topics are covered, although the literary pieces used differ when a high-quality literary translation into Spanish does not exist for the text required in the English mainstream course. In that case, an appropriate text is chosen in a Spanish original.

In U.S. history, challenging curriculum has also been translated into Spanish. In 1994, the school decided to purchase Teachers Curriculum Institute (TCI) materials, a set of curricula and instructional strategies designed by former social studies teachers to help social studies teachers reach students from diverse academic backgrounds. The TCI curriculum emphasizes experiential and reflective learning, case studies, role playing, and lessons embedded in sensory support through the use of multimedia. The original English versions of these materials are used in the English and sheltered classes, while the Spanish translation is used in the Spanish classes.

Books for science and other subjects are purchased in Mexico whenever their content is aligned with the California curriculum frameworks. When this is not possible, the books used in class are in English, but the class discussion occurs in Spanish. All of these arrangements are based on the belief Calexico teachers share that academic understandings need to be conducted in a language the students understand. If deep conceptual understanding in science is developed in Spanish, for example, then after the students have acquired enough English, these conceptual understandings can be used in English. Furthermore, if the types of activities that students engage in while studying in Spanish are used while studying in English, students will be familiar with the structure of the task and be able to focus on the content.

The senior project

In 1993, Calexico High School introduced the senior project as a graduation requirement, a three-part project that engages students in

- writing a research paper on a topic of their choice;
- applying the knowledge and skills acquired during their research and general education to the development of a product or to involvement in some action (e.g., students may build a model to scale, tutor elementary school students, or volunteer in a hospital); and
- making an oral presentation to a board of judges to demonstrate their knowledge and skills, integrating the academic and experiential components of the project. The board of judges, a committee formed by five adults, three teachers and two community members, question students to assess the depth of their academic and applied knowledge.

(Calexico High School, 1993)

The senior project, a performance-based evaluation of knowledge and competence, combines research with reading, writing, listening, and speaking in various contexts and registers. As students develop their projects, they establish goals, plan their work, carry it out, and monitor themselves. As they research their topics, they need to demonstrate appropriate understanding of the conventions of research such as formulating a question to investigate, checking a variety of sources, presenting findings in a variety of formats, and creating a bibliography. The project also requires that students be in close contact with an adult mentor, an expert in the field the student is exploring, who may be a teacher or a person from the community. This component increases communication between students, staff, and the community. Finally, during the exhibition (the public defense of the project), after having gone through considerable preparation, students have the opportunity to demonstrate their expertise in front of adults and to practice their communication skills in formal situations.

The senior project is written and presented in English if the student is in ESL III or at a higher level of English proficiency. If the student is enrolled in an ESL I or II class, the project is written and presented in Spanish with the same requirements otherwise. (This alternative does not satisfy everybody in the community, as will be discussed later.) Whether the project is developed in English or in Spanish, students still benefit from the same process and develop the same integrated skills. The project encourages students to pursue a topic of interest and become knowledgeable about it. It teaches them to challenge themselves, cope with the pressure of deadlines, monitor their own progress, prepare themselves for performance in the real world, and assess their own performance—competencies that all young people ought to have in any language. If these skills are developed in students' primary language, they can be transferred to English with minimal support needed, once a threshold level of proficiency in English is reached. When the transfer occurs, students will be able to perform critical tasks with efficiency in two languages.

A great deal of thought and work is invested in students' development of their projects. During my second visit to Calexico High School in May of 1995, I observed a session in which a teacher was advising a student on how to produce her presentation. Eréndira, a student in ESL III, had chosen to study the process of digital and traditional photographic development. She initially conducted some library research and then did an apprenticeship with a well-known photographer from the community. She had documented her learning process in writing and with a video. She was now in the computer laboratory learning to edit her demonstration video with the help of her project tutor, Mr. Méndez. On the day that I observed the process, Eréndira and Mr. Méndez worked collaboratively for almost 2 hours. They had had several other sessions together before, and they would meet again before the project was finished. For Eréndira and the other seniors, these mentoring sessions personalize their education, providing time with teachers that probably would not have been available without the requirement of the project.

Eréndira treasured this time with her mentor. It gave her considerable individual time with a teacher she respected and an opportunity to develop her communicative repertoire in English as she discussed, reformulated, and advanced her project with him. As she said to me:

I have invested many hours in this project already, but it is very exciting. For some students, the difficult part is choosing a topic that will be enticing enough for them to want to spend the time with it. For me, that was no problem. I had always been intrigued by photography, and the project gave me the opportunity to find out about it. I have learned so much—about the photographic process, to develop films, to produce a video, to edit sequences. I have learned a lot of new concepts and the words to talk about them in English—actually, in Spanish, too.

Eréndira's project combined Spanish and English in a fluid, logical, and efficient way. Her library research was conducted in English, but interactions with the photographer took place in Spanish because he felt more comfortable talking about his craft in Spanish. Work with Mr. Méndez was conducted in English because it was geared to the presentation, which was to take place in English. The paper was written in English. For the video production, however, Eréndira made use of her Spanish every time the photographer spoke because she had to voice over his explanations in Spanish, interpreting in English for her audience. She did this with admirable proficiency. In a similar fashion, many of her peers moved back and forth comfortably between the two languages as they developed their projects. Most of them combined bibliographic work in English with field work in Spanish, which was then reflected on, analyzed, and reported in English. As Hakuta (1993) and others have noted, the translation and interpretation abilities of many immigrant students are on par with the abilities displayed by international interpreters and deserve to be valued, promoted, and enhanced in the educational system.

As Ancess and Darling-Hammond (1995) note in their study of the senior project at Hodgson Vocational/Technical High School, senior projects benefit both students and teachers. They provide learning and language development opportunities for students, while at the same time creating major changes in the nature of teachers' everyday work, expanding their roles and promoting collaboration among teachers. These changes can be very exciting, but if not properly prepared for, they can also cause strain, as is discussed below.

Counseling

Academies in 10th grade, taught by a team of teachers, allow for an efficient system of counseling. A few counselors are in charge of specific clusters of students and can be in contact with the same team of teachers whenever the need arises. In this way, difficulties can be addressed early. The support provided by the counselors ranges from interventions designed to sustain or improve academic success, to coordination with agencies outside the school that provide social services needed for learning. Counselors and teachers at Calexico High School aggressively encourage graduation and postsecondary education options for students. In fact, Calexico High School ranks very well among schools in the state in graduation rates, fulfillment of A–F requirements (needed for application to the University of California system), and enrollment in higher education.

Years ago, however, Calexico High staff did not have high expectations for all of their students. As previously mentioned, immigrant students who had little or no proficiency in English were not given the opportunity to study challenging content and pursue educational goals beyond high school. Mr. Cervantes, a former student and now an excellent math teacher at the school, was dissuaded by teachers and counselors from considering high-level math courses and university studies. He had always been good at mathematics and wanted to become a mathematics teacher, but no school staff supported his interest or guided him in the right direction. After graduating from high school, he became a truck driver. After several years on this job, still nurturing the dream of helping youngsters develop competence in and enthusiasm for math, he quit and applied for a teacher's aide position in an elementary school. He did extremely well in this capacity. He loved teaching, and the students appreciated his commitment and his teaching. On many occasions he was in charge of the class, although there was a certified teacher in the room who was the designated classroom teacher. Mr. Cervantes's understanding of second language learners and his ability to adapt his teaching to them made him popular with teachers and students at the school. School personnel encouraged him to study at the university to get his teaching credential. He did so, and he has been a teacher for many years, most of them at Calexico High.

Many teachers who studied in Calexico schools and as second language learners suffered the inequities of low expectations and the tracking system, have a personal commitment to making sure that education now serves the needs of all students. In a survey conducted by Richard Neumann (1996), who was interested in the low student dropout rate in Calexico, youth were asked, in an open-ended format, to "describe the two most important things about Calexico High School that make students want to stay in school." The most frequent response (40%) was that teachers were interested in students, cared for them, and motivated them continuously. The second most frequent response (38%) was that the school atmosphere made students believe that they could succeed. This commitment is consistent with the mission of the district, which has model bilingual schools at the elementary school level, and it reaffirms the culture of equity that the school and the community profess.

Curricular Progression for English Learners

English language learners at Calexico High School take 2 periods of ESL daily. Although the goal in both periods is to develop overall communicative competence in English, including its conversational and academic aspects, one period emphasizes the development of oral skills and the other, written English. This focus reflects the need to work on students' ability to write a variety of texts in English, a need that has become more pressing with the creation of the senior project.

The program requires that students in ESL I, the beginning course in English, take their main subject area courses in Spanish. At this level of English proficiency, students interact with their English-speaking peers in physical education, arts, or foreign language classes. ESL II students take sheltered English math and science, and literature and social studies in Spanish. As students reach ESL III, the advanced level of English as a second language, they are mainstreamed into most of their subject matter courses and take sheltered literature and social studies.

This is the plan at Calexico High School. At times, however, not all required courses are taught in their sheltered versions or are not offered several times throughout the day to enable participation by all students at an intermediate level of competence in English. In some instances, students who should be taking a sheltered English course take the course in Spanish instead. From an academic point of view this is fine because they do not miss concepts and competencies they should develop. However, in addition to developing subject matter expertise, sheltered classes develop subject matter communicative competence in English. This is not possible when sheltered offerings are limited. When compared to courses offered by other schools in California, however, Calexico High School has the most varied array of offerings in primary language and sheltered instruction.

Instructional Practices

At Calexico High School, teachers vary widely in their pedagogical practices, which range from the traditional teacher-fronted classroom where transmission of ideas is the goal, to highly interactive, learner-centered, constructivist classes. There is a growing—although not general—recognition among teachers at Calexico High School that professional development is needed to reorient their practice and make it effective for all students.

I visited four ESL classes because I was interested in seeing how these classes were conducted and in observing whether separate ESL periods for oral and written skill development worked. In fact, teachers confided that they did not pay much attention to the course nomenclature, and that they combined speaking, listening, reading, and writing tasks in all of their classes. Teachers wanted their students to read texts, react to them, make predictions, act out scenes, and so on. A well-selected reading provided the focus, perspective, and language for these oral explorations. Having established a variety of oral language activities, the next logical step was to engage students in writing activities that would enable them to revisit the same topic and language previously practiced, via a different skill and with a different purpose and different audiences. The following vignette profiles one course I observed in depth.

ESL II with Mr. Pachter

In Mr. Pachter's ESL II (Intermediate) class, supposedly the oral section, students were getting ready to read *The Outsiders* (Hinton, 1967). Students were asked to do a quick write (a brief period of free writing) in response to a scenario presented by the teacher. The scenario was intended to help students imagine a situation similar to the one that Ponyboy, the main character in the book, faced at the beginning of the story, and react to it. Mr. Pachter dramatically described his scene. Students listened attentively, pencils in hand, ready to respond. After giving them a few minutes to write, Mr. Pachter asked them to "pair and share" their reactions orally. He then asked a few students to share their answers with the whole class. After four students shared, he started reading the book aloud, stopping to check for comprehension. Four minutes into the reading, at an exciting moment in the story, Mr. Pachter stopped and asked the students to speculate, in dyads, about what they thought would happen next. With several possibilities volunteered by students, once again Mr. Pachter distributed the books and asked the students to read a page silently to compare their predictions with what happened in the story. Throughout the class and the next day, this type of interactive reading continued. Sometimes students discussed assigned questions in dyads or groups of four. At other times they explored alternatives to the actions of characters in the story. Sometimes they reacted to visualizations, richly described scenes that Mr. Pachter presented orally for the students to react to.

During my second visit to this class, students seated in groups of five played "hot seat," an activity in which one student assumes the personality of one of the characters in the story and responds in character to the questions that group members ask regarding actions, thoughts, and feelings.

I was curious about why Mr. Pachter chose *The Outsiders* for this class and how he viewed the teaching of literature as part of the development of English proficiency. He explained that he chose it partly for its content.

The students relate to this novel. The human issues it deals with, gangs, family misunderstandings, love, solidarity—all of them are real issues for my kids. I really want to touch their lives, and this book does that.

He chose it partly because of what ESL II students could learn from reading books that were difficult for them.

I want them to know that they can understand the big ideas in a novel without necessarily comprehending every word in the text. At first that is a bit difficult because they want to check in the dictionary for every word that they do not know. This to me is an essential skill, to go for broader understandings and to guess at the meaning of words from the context.

Finally, he chose it because he wanted them to become good readers.

I try to get students to predict because that is something that good readers do naturally, without giving it much thought. One thing I like to do is have students predict, based on information provided in the text. This is all part of making connections. Their writing in my class is connected to making sense of what they are reading and discussing.

For this teacher, the ESL class is a vehicle for getting students to explore real life issues, develop strategies that good readers possess, write to understand text, talk to explore relevant topics, and above all expand their linguistic, study, and life skills.

The Challenges of School-Based Change

Calexico High School has a core of strongly committed teachers who are willing to volunteer time and effort beyond their normal work schedule and who want to use any means possible to promote the success of the English learners in the school. There is a second group of teachers who, although they do not volunteer to work on the restructuring of the school, support efforts in that direction. Finally, there is a small group of teachers who are dissatisfied with the way things are at the school and who have concerns about teaching subject matter courses in Spanish. These teachers feel that in an American secondary school, students should be taking all their coursework in English. When

I asked one of them how a recently arrived student with little English proficiency would understand the classroom language, his answer was, "Well, they should."

Implementation of restructuring principles is not always successful; the road to change is paved with politics. The changes taking place at Calexico High created a sense of fractionalization that illustrates one of the dilemmas of change: how to involve everybody at the school site in a positive way. Unless everybody participates, the process can be delayed, and there is a danger of losing the initial momentum and direction. If only a core of committed, visionary teachers takes the lead, they are perceived as an "in-group" and not necessarily legitimate representatives of the school. This dilemma has arisen in many school change efforts. In a study of eight schools in the Coalition of Essential Schools (CES), Muncey and McQuillan (1993) found that engagement in the process of change revealed deep and irreconcilable differences in teachers' philosophical, pedagogical, and personal ideologies. Furthermore, in schools where not all the teachers chose to embrace CES ideas, those who did embrace them formed an in-group, which divided the faculty. The out-group members then maintained, "and usually correctly, that Coalition teachers had fewer students, better students, lighter teaching loads, and more free periods and that they received a disproportionate amount of professional development funds" and compensated release time (Muncey & McQuillan, 1993, p. 488).

How did this dilemma play out at Calexico High School? Initially, all teachers were invited to participate in the discussions that lead to the creation of the academies and institutes. These sessions, however, usually took place during regular teaching hours, and teachers did not want to miss classes. An alternative to working sporadically throughout the academic year was to work in more concentrated ways during the summer, as two groups of teachers did, developing units that integrate themes across subjects. For most teachers, however, the idea of working during the summer was not enticing. As a consequence, the same group of teachers usually ended up participating voluntarily in these activities, thus reinforcing a feeling of factionalization within the school.

The first of 3 years of restructuring efforts consisted of reformulating the larger structural units of the school: detracking, creating institutes and academies, developing curricula, and a brief attempt at block scheduling. In an article discussing the limited impact of school reform on educational practice, Richard F. Elmore (1995) suggested three main reasons for restructuring schools in structural ways: it has high symbolic value, that is, it communicates a sense that change is serious; as difficult as it is to change structures, "they are easier than most other candidates for change" (p. 24); there is also a strong sense that the existing structures constrain educators' ability to work effectively with students. Elmore proposed that reforms might concentrate first on "changing norms, knowledge, and skills at the individual and organizational level before focusing on changing structure. That is, teachers might actually learn to teach differently and develop shared expectations and beliefs about what good teaching is, and then invent the organizational structures that go with those shared skills, expectations, and beliefs" (p. 26).

With structural changes in place at Calexico High, however, it became evident that changes in vision and pedagogical practices did not automatically follow. Teachers realized that they needed to focus attention on developing a common vision of what powerful learning at the school could look like, which is partly why they instituted the senior project. The senior project was to be a catalyst for focusing on the abilities students needed to engage in research and produce extended pieces of written discourse related to various disciplines. Whether this occurred in English or in Spanish, teachers felt it needed to be a high-quality process that rendered high-quality products.

Detracking of math courses made it clear that teachers needed to rethink their approaches to the teaching of subject areas. The first year that all math courses were college preparatory courses, the number of students failing them increased. The expectations for what students needed to achieve had changed, but the ways of engaging students in the development of their academic ability also needed to change so that more students could succeed. This is a serious issue in restructuring. Schools and districts cannot just change structures and requirements and expect that teachers' and students' work will fulfill the new expectations. Calexico High School staff still need to resolve this issue.

In addition to the deliberate modifications listed above, in 1993 another major change affected the culture of the school. The ninth graders became part of the newly built middle school to relieve overcrowding at the high school. This move created a number of repercussions at the high school: A group of very committed teachers were now middle school teachers, and teachers at the high school perceived that the maturity level of incoming 10th graders dropped. These teachers felt that the first year in a high school marks a transitional stage for students between being immature teenagers and more responsible high schoolers, which they are supposed to be by the 10th grade. This belief is in synch with a generalized notion in this country that developmentally, students in Grades 6, 7, and 8 "have more in common in terms of physical, psychological, social and intellectual variables than do those in other age–grade combinations" (*Caught in the Middle,* 1993), and that students in Grade 9 tend to identify emotionally and intellectually with students in Grades 10 through 12. Without exposure on campus to these higher grades, ninth graders were not becoming prepared for the high school culture. With the 1993 change, a process of transition and adjustment that had taken place in the 9th grade was postponed until the 10th grade, and teachers needed to prepare responses to alleviate the situation.

As a result, closer coordination between the high school and the new middle school began, facilitated by the presence of former high school teachers at the new middle school site. High school students also began working with middle school students and giving them advice about high school life and commitments.

As a consequence of these changes, the staff at Calexico High School decided to concentrate their efforts on professional growth for the years 1995-96 and 1996-97. Their two-pronged strategy included days in which teachers would work on their pedagogical practices by: (1) participating in sessions in which they model, reflect on, and apply ways of helping their students construct their own understandings by jointly developing curricula for the teaching of subject matter; and (2) working together to develop performance criteria and rubrics to implement these criteria appropriately during the teaching of their courses. The purpose of this work was to establish the pedagogical vision and guidelines that would underlie the Spanish classes for students beginning their development of English, sheltered content classes for students at an intermediate level of proficiency in English, and mainstream classes for students with sufficient English proficiency. The standards and the vision for these courses are intended to be the same. The variation lies in the linguistic format of the offerings.

Conclusion

Calexico High is a special place because most of its inhabitants are either bilingual in Spanish and English or are in the process of becoming so. The original decision of school staff to concentrate their reform efforts on changing the structures of the school to facilitate the promotion of higher academic standards for all, regardless of language, is being complemented with an emphasis on retooling teachers' instructional understandings and practices.

The local context presents the school with advantages and disadvantages. On one hand, having parallel courses in English, Spanish, and sheltered English is easier where students speak either Spanish or English than in schools with immigrant students from varied cultural and linguistic backgrounds. Finding teachers that can teach courses in sophisticated Spanish is not a problem, either, since these teachers live in the community. On the other hand, the possibility for the teachers to develop into a community of practitioners with shared beliefs, values, and practices may take a longer time because the school is so large.

Teachers will need to develop a collective understanding over time by engaging in important discussions about their everyday practices and educational goals.

The characteristics of the community itself present advantages and disadvantages to the implementation of educational reform. Because it is a bilingual community, there is a shared understanding of the value and importance of becoming bilingual. However, some teachers feel that students in the community are overprotected and lack a clear sense of the linguistic tensions present in the rest of the state and the country. The high level of unemployment in the community contributes to a sense that education does not necessarily open doors for everybody. It also lessens the possibility of establishing school-to-work programs that can make education more relevant for many students.

A frequently discussed issue is whether students should graduate before having mastered English. This question is not easily answered. Because it is a border town, Calexico continuously receives immigrant students. Sometimes their age makes 11th or 12th grade an appropriate placement, but they have no English background. How can they gain enough proficiency in English to research, implement, and publicly defend the senior project in this language after only 1 or 2 years of schooling? For the time being, the local community college continues the development of English skills that the high school starts, although representatives of the California Community College system are already discussing whether this is the right institution to develop English language skills.

Another issue that Calexico High raises is whether a large school can change harmoniously. Given the structural features of high schools discussed in chapter 3, it seems almost unimaginable that a large institution can succeed in comprehensive restructuring. Smaller high schools may be an idea whose time has come.

Calexico High School teachers also experimented briefly with the restructuring of time by implementing a system of block schedules in which students enrolled in three courses every semester, as opposed to six. The decision to move from a traditional to a block schedule was hastily and enthusiastically made by a group of teachers. The advantages were obvious to them: Every day they would see half the number of students they regularly worked with, diminishing considerably the amount of homework to correct; they could get to know their students better and give them more support. However, time was not devoted to discussing the pedagogical implications of having a double period every day, nor were all teachers, students, and community members informed about the changes and their rationale. The experience at Calexico High School sends a strong cautionary note to teachers at other sites interested in the same change. When the new school year started and some teachers were not ready for it, students started complaining about the change. Not everybody at the school was equally ready to defend the choice to the students, and after a brief trial and a student demonstration that took students to the district office, the schedule went back to the traditional 6 daily periods.

Despite these limitations and the difficulties of school restructuring, Calexico High School has, through the commitment and willingness to change that many of its teachers display, managed to create a highly effective secondary school program for many immigrant students. Their efforts are especially admirable given the sink-or-swim approach to immigrant students' education that used to be pervasive in this school.

Materials Available

- Math I and II College Preparatory Math (CPM) materials translated into Spanish
- U.S. History TCI (Teachers Curriculum Institute) translated into Spanish (10th grade)
- Senior project information in English and Spanish
- College application information in English and Spanish
- Achievement Via Individual Determination (AVID) materials in English and Spanish

Contact

Calexico High School
1030 Encinas Avenue
Calexico CA 92231
Phone (760) 357-7440
Fax (760) 357-9640

International High School, Long Island City, New York—A Focus on Instructional Practices and Curriculum Integration

Since its founding in 1985, International High School has established itself as one of the premier schools for immigrant students. The staff have designed an innovative, student-centered program based on interdisciplinary study, a commitment to teaching challenging academic content to English language learners, and a significant focus on career education. This exciting program continues to evolve and grow, and its graduates continue to experience tremendous success in language, academic, and personal growth.

The Setting

For many people, both in the United States and abroad, New York City conjures up images of the Statue of Liberty, opening the country's doors to immigrants and visitors from all corners of the world. The city has been one of the most active ports of entry for people wishing to establish themselves in this country, and consequently, it has always been associated with a rich variety of languages, ethnicities, and customs, and a general openness to difference. This ethnic and linguistic variety has provided the perfect setting for International High School, located in the borough of Queens.

The School

International High School (IHS) has become synonymous with innovation, high standards, and success for its exclusively immigrant population. When people hear about International High School, where over 90% of the students pass the statewide Regents Competency Tests, and 90% of the graduates go on to postsecondary education, they imagine an exclusive and comfortable preparatory school for privileged foreign students. Nothing could be further from the truth. Over 75% of the students enrolled at International qualify for free or reduced-price lunch. The school does not have a building for itself, occupying instead several classrooms in the basement of LaGuardia Community College. However, these factors, which initially surprise uninitiated visitors, are counterbalanced by the energy, enthusiasm, *esprit de corps*, and involvement of teachers and students alike. During the 1994-95 academic year, International High School had 450 students who had immigrated from 56 countries and spoke 40 different languages. The largest group of students comes from Spanish-speaking countries, followed by Asian countries represented by China, Hong Kong, Bangladesh, India, Pakistan, and Afghanistan. Enrollment at the high school reflects the geopolitics of the moment, with many students coming from places in turmoil (Richardson, 1993). When the school opened in 1985, only a few students were from Eastern Europe; in 1995, Eastern European students were the third largest group.

International High School, part of the Alternative School System of New York City, is a joint venture of the New York City Board of Education and the City University of New York. During its brief existence, IHS has repeatedly earned recognition. In 1986, International and its partner, the City University of New York, received the award for the Best New High School/College Collaboration in the nation from the Council for Advancement and Support of Education. In 1989, the National Council of Teachers of English gave the school its award for excellence in English/Language Arts Instruction, and in 1990 the same organization named International a Center of Excellence for At-Risk Students. In 1991, the American Association of Higher Education gave the school its award for Outstanding High School/College Collaboration. In 1992, it received a Democracy grant from R.J.R. Nabisco and a National Academic Excellence award from the U.S. Department of Education.

Every year, 92% to 95% of IHS's recent graduates apply for and are accepted to college. Two thirds attend 4-year colleges; one third attend 2-year colleges. Eighty percent of those going on to 4-year institutions attend City University of New York, and 20% enroll in state or private colleges. The colleges that International alumni attended in 1994 include Alfred, Bard, Barnard, Buffalo College, Clark, New Paltz, New York University, Pace, St. John's, Skidmore, Stony Brook, the University of Washington at Seattle, and Vanderbilt. These students received 4-year financial aid packages totaling $750,000 (International Schools Partnership, n.d., pp. 26-27).

Because IHS occupies space at LaGuardia Community College, nothing can be left behind in the classrooms at the end of the day because college classes occupy the same premises in the evening. This condition, which would discourage teachers in other settings, does not diminish the spirit of the school and its staff: They have turned around conditions that under normal circumstances would be considered stumbling blocks, or at least distractions, and have made strengths out of them. If being housed at LaGuardia Community College does not give the school a permanent campus of its own, it offers students and teachers many other advantages. The ethnic composition of the college is also very diverse, with about 30% Latino students, 20% Eastern European, 30% Asian, and 20% Anglo American or other ethnicities The high school students are surrounded by college students with language and cultural backgrounds similar to their own who can serve as role models, and they have the opportunity to interact with them daily.

School Culture

The mission of International High School is for each of its students to develop the linguistic, cognitive, and cultural skills necessary for success in high school, college, and beyond. The principles that undergird the program, as stated in school documents (see International High School, 1993, p. 2), are as follows:

- Limited English proficient students require the ability to understand, speak, read, and write English with near-native fluency to realize their full potential within an English-speaking society.

- In an increasingly interdependent world, fluency in a language other than English must not be viewed as a handicap, but rather as a resource for the student, the school, and the society.
- Language skills are most effectively learned in context and embedded in a content area.
- The most successful educational programs are those that emphasize high expectations coupled with effective support systems.
- Attempts to group students homogeneously in an effort to make instruction more manageable prevent students from learning in the way in which individuals learn best, that is, from each other.
- The carefully planned use of multiple learning contexts in addition to the classroom (e.g., learning centers, career internship sites, field trips), facilitates language acquisition and content area mastery.
- Career education is a significant motivational factor for adolescent learners.
- The most effective instruction takes place when teachers actively participate in the school decision-making process, including instructional program design, curriculum development, and materials selection.

These principles are evident in the everyday life of the school. One hears a variety of languages spoken in and out of class, but one also hears English in classes and in corridors. As one eavesdrops, the topics of conversation strike the listener as being far more serious and elaborated than the interactions one usually hears in school halls. For example, I observed three students, one of them Polish and two Latin Americans, discussing the Cuban embargo. One Latino was a Castro sympathizer, while the other one opposed his actions, and the Polish student, wanting to become better informed, kept probing both of them with extremely critical questions.

Intake and Exit Procedures

To be admitted to International High School, a student needs to have lived in the United States fewer than 4 years and to score below the 21st percentile on the Language Assessment Battery. Once admitted, the student remains at the high school until graduation, since there are no exit procedures other than graduation. The school does not have a transitional program to move youth into other educational settings. Students who, in other schools, would be mainstreamed into English-only classes when they have achieved a high level of English proficiency remain at IHS and become key actors in a highly interactive distributed expertise model, in which they are the more capable linguistic peers in a Vygotskyan fashion (Vygotsky, 1978, p. 86).

Some of the students arrive with low literacy skills in their primary language and with little prior schooling; a few are beyond the traditional age for high school. Others come with strong academic backgrounds in their primary language, but with limited proficiency in English. Still others have transferred from traditional schools where they were not doing well academically or socially. Most of these students heard about the school through friends, relatives, or their counselors. It is a popular school with a waiting list for admission that works on a first come, first served basis. Once admitted, students are told that they will spend at least 2 years at school before graduation because school staff believe that it will take them that long to adjust to the system and the language. (D. Hirschy, personal communication, May 15, 1995)

By the time students graduate, they have completed their credits, including a half-day work internship conducted during 3 academic quarters, and 75% of them have taken one or more college courses. More importantly, they have learned to become autonomous learners through experiential, metacognitive, and collaborative learning. They have also learned to appreciate rich linguistic and cultural diversity and to discuss openly their possibilities for the future in such a society.

The Staff

International High School was founded by a group of like-minded teachers under the visionary leadership of Eric Nadelstern, the principal. All teachers had previously taught in more traditional schools and had had immigrant students in their classes. Dissatisfied with the way things had worked elsewhere, they shared a common vision of what was possible and decided to work to realize this vision.

All teachers at International are firm believers in bilingualism as an individual gift and a societal resource. They also believe that immigrant students can not only learn English through engagement in subject matter taught in that language, but can also, if provided with the appropriate support, excel academically. In contrast to most other high school teachers, the staff at IHS are interested not only in perfecting their specialization in one area but in extending their expertise beyond their original subjects. After all, interdisciplinary teaching requires them to continuously learn with their peers to facilitate learning for their students. As Aaron Listhaus, a teacher at International, confided in the introduction to his self-evaluation (written self-evaluations are done annually by all school staff) in May of 1995,

According to the National Alliance for Restructuring Education, maximum learning, as defined by meaningful retention as well as personal interest, takes place when one actually teaches the learning to someone else. Thus I have learned more this year about teaching and learning from working with my students, team members and student teachers than I have ever before. This year in general and this cycle to a larger degree, I have been team teaching across disciplines with both team members and student teachers. Because of the collaboration, the observation of differing styles and personal dynamics, dealing with subjects as outwardly disparate as Art, Mathematics, Biology, Chemistry, Global Studies, Linguistics, and Language Arts, I have been a part of many diverse learning situations.

Teachers at International have developed a process for peer selection, support, and evaluation that strongly resembles the processes they engage their students in as they work through the various interdisciplinary curriculum units (described below). This process is designed to foster and support professional growth on the part of the teacher through self and peer evaluation. (See also the discussion of professional development at International High School in González & Darling-Hammond, 1997, pp. 110-119.)

Instructional Practices: Interdisciplinary Units

The design of instruction at International has been evolving since its inception. Initially, although there was a strong belief in the value of cross-disciplinary work to enhance teaching and learning at the school, classes were divided along disciplinary lines, and the links between disciplines were tenuous. Students had seven 35- to 40-minute classes a day. For the 1988-89 academic year, International adopted a new schedule based on a 70-minute instructional period. The schedule change was positive and created the possibility for serious cross-disciplinary teaching.

Believing that the departmentalization of our secondary schools has led to fragmentation of learning (as discussed in chapter 3), the staff at International have created interdisciplinary units to unify and connect knowledge for students while helping to build small learning communities. Planning for these units, or "clusters," has also benefited the teachers, who plan their instruction collaboratively based on their students' interests and needs. This interdisciplinary approach has been so successful that the faculty of International have decided to "reorganize the curriculum of the entire school around interdisciplinary thematic study" (International High School, 1993, p. 10). These clusters, listed below, have been carefully designed so that they provide students with the conceptual understandings, academic skills, and credits they will need in order to graduate and to pass the Regents competency tests.

Twelve interdisciplinary clusters have been developed by International High School teachers. Each is taught during a 13-week period so that students enroll in three clusters during an academic year. The clusters are not sequenced in any particularl way, although conceptual connections are made within and across them. There is a commonly held belief that sequential order is necessary in the teaching of certain subjects, but teachers at International are not convinced of its validity. Their experience with these clusters—which are continuously being refined—has convinced them to the contrary, that in fact the traditional sequencing of concepts within a discipline limits students' possibilities to see the connections that can be drawn between and across concepts. Table 4 shows the interdisciplinary clusters taught at International High School when I visited in 1995.

Table 4. Interdisciplinary Clusters and Their Component Disciplines at International High School, 1995

Interdisciplinary Clusters	Disciplines
American Reality	Career/Occupational Education Internships Foreign Language (Native Language Arts) (Human Development)
Beginnings (Origins)	Art English Mathematics Science
Conflict Resolution	American Studies Mathematics Art Career/Occupational Education
Crime and Punishment	English American Studies Mathematics
Visibility, Invisibility	English Physical Education (Project Adventure) Science
World Around Us	American Studies or Global Studies Mathematics Science
American Dream	American Studies Career/Occupational Education English Music
It's Your World	Art English Mathematics Science
Motion	English Physical Education (Project Adventure) Science

(Table 4 continues on the next page.)

Table 4 *(continued)*

Interdisciplinary Clusters	Disciplines
Structures	Global Studies Language Arts Mathematics Science
21st Century	English Global Studies Mathematics
World of Money	American Studies English Mathematics Science

The following profiles illuminate how these interdisciplinary clusters function on a daily basis.

Global Studies

The first class I visited at International was the Global Studies component of the *Structures* interdisciplinary cluster. Students were completing a 2-week research project on World Religions, which had been developed by Karen Reuter and Brenda Lapley, two student teachers from the New School for Social Research in collaboration with International High School teachers Charles Glassman, Elyse Rivin, and Aaron Listhaus. The project combines global studies and art. At the beginning of the project, students were asked to select a religion unfamiliar to them and to become experts on that religion; they were also asked to create or recreate a religious artifact from this religion and to explain in an oral presentation the significant features and history of the object. They had conducted the research project in dyads. Each student had gone to a museum that exhibited religious artifacts to support the activity and to help contextualize the research. Students were not given specific questions to answer but were told that they were free to study any aspect of the religion that triggered their curiosity. Some students chose to focus on the historical events leading to the birth and evolution of the religion, while others chose to learn about current issues, practices, and customs. To kick off the project, students watched scenes from the film *Little Buddha* (Bertolucci, 1993-94), and then in groups of four brainstormed questions that could serve as a guide for their own research. The questions were gathered together and distributed to the class to provide support to students who needed more direction. Some of their questions were "Is there really a god? Why do people pray? What is the religion's creation story? Has the religion changed over time? Does the religion have hope?"

A few days before the project was completed, students worked with a partner who had been studying a different religion, and they interviewed each other about their research. This interview served two purposes: to inform every student in class about a religion they had not researched and to assess informally the quality of each student's work. Questions that were not clearly explained or remained unanswered in the interviews could now be used to better define the scope of the work or to provide further lines of inquiry for the remaining days.

When I arrived, on the last day of the second week of this project, the students were preparing for the final presentation, which was to take place during the sixth period that day. The student pairs sat at tables of six, sharing their findings with other classmates who had studied different religions. At the table I joined, a student who had studied Islam started his presentation by explaining his reasons for researching this religion. Looking at a chart of important religions in the world, he had realized that Islam was the second most popular religion in the world after Christianity, and he decided that he needed to know more about it. He had also heard about a movement called "The Nation of Islam" and wanted to know whether this referred to the religion or to a political party. He went on to explain what he had learned in the process, while everybody listened intently. The only time a voice from outside the circle intervened, it was to remind eager students that they should reserve their questions for the end of each presentation. Four groups were sharing their studies at the same time, and the concentrated attention at each circle indicated that everybody was thoroughly involved in the process. As questions came up, students responded to them by providing the requested information, or by saying that their study had not concentrated on the issues addressed by the questions and restating the focus of their research.

The culminating activity of the project, conducted during the sixth period, was an informal conversation held in another small-group configuration so that students could learn about other religions and about religion in general. This time, at each table five or six students sat with their artifacts and with an adult—a teacher, a student teacher, a teacher aide, or a visitor—ready to engage in a discussion. These conversations clearly revealed what students had learned during their research projects. Although students had their carefully constructed written reports with them, they could not rely on them for their initial presentation or during the discussion. As Aaron Listhaus explained to me,

They had to rely solely upon what they had remembered, and what they had remembered was what was important to them. Because this conversation was spontaneous and since we had allotted a double period for the event, those students who might have been nervous about speaking extemporaneously to a small group had the time to relax and prepare what they had wanted to say. I believe that this method of assessment is accurate and fair, while supporting the particular needs of each student. By the end of the conversation, each student felt relaxed and felt that they had demonstrated what they had learned and how hard they had worked.

The written part of the project consisted of a report, an essay, or a poster. The only instructions were to demonstrate what they had learned and to use their own words.

The following aspects of the World Religions project make it especially enticing for students and help them have access to, and become engaged in, higher order learning:

• **Choice**: At the beginning of the project, students were given ample time and resources to find a religion that would really interest them and that would therefore sustain their enthusiasm and hard work through the 2 weeks of the project.

• **Focus and building from prior knowledge**: Once a religion was chosen, students collaboratively generated questions that could guide their research. For those students who already had a focus, this helped to sharpen it. For those students who had not selected an area of interest to pursue, this brainstorming activity provided them with possibilities.

• **Collaboration**: A large portion of the research was conducted in dyads, which allowed students to support each other's learning, both conceptually and linguistically, as they engaged in purposeful activities. At other times, the students worked in groups of four or five, which led to the sharing and refinement of understandings. During these interactions, the atmosphere in the classroom was supportive rather than competitive. All students participated orally; all of them took notes. There were no simplistic role divisions that maximized learning for some while restricting it for others.

• **Validation of all languages**: Although it was clearly understood by all that English needs to be developed by all students, it was also clear that other languages are equally important in the construction and negotiation of meaning. Once in a while, students used their native languages to discuss, clarify, or expand ideas related to the project.

• **Distributed expertise**: Students were asked to become experts on a religion of their choice, and throughout the project, opportunities were provided them to tell their peers what they were learning, share their expertise, and receive feedback. Research was a vehicle for establishing meaningful conversations about focused, common themes of interest that allowed all students to share their emerging knowledge and contribute to everybody's understandings.

• **Emphasis on quality, in-depth work**: By the end of the project, all students had gained in-depth knowledge of one religion and had had ample opportunities to assess their development of this expertise, refining and strengthening the focus of their research.

• **Heterogeneity**: Students were free to choose their teammates within certain parameters that were shared and understood by all. As Natalia, a Puerto Rican student, told me,

When a student is new to English and needs more support, partners come from their same language background so that they can help them understand the intricacies of a text. As students become more adept in English, it becomes more important to work with students from other language backgrounds so that they have to use their English.

At other times, students formed groups to share different types of expertise. In general there were "high and varied expectations for each individual (and) creative support systems (that) aid students in accomplishing these expectations" (International High School, 1993, p. 20). The final written product, for example, could be a report, an essay, or a poster. This was left for the students to choose, but the variety provided students with less fluency in English an opportunity to demonstrate their understandings through less extensive written discourse. Students could also hand in an essay written in another language, if there was an adult available at the school to read that language.

• **Multidisciplinary focus**: As students worked to produce oral and written presentations of their work, they were engaged in finding historical patterns that underlie the many religions of the world. Their religious objects provided a way of contextualizing and comparing their understandings of similarities and differences in the way religions are structured. In other classes—science, literature, and math—students would also look at the persistence of similar patterns through other topics and disciplines. The theme allowed students to analyze and grasp the connections that run through what otherwise might seem like unrelated issues.

World of Money

The World of Money cluster focuses on a study of the role and impact of economics through historical time and geographical space, and it incorporates American studies, English literature, mathematics, and science. To highlight how International maintains high expectations for all learners at all levels of English proficiency, I show below three extracts from students' responses to an assignment on the novel *Thousand Pieces of Gold* (McCunn, 1981). Students were asked to (a) provide a brief summary of the book, (b) analyze the economic, social, and political implications of the theme, and (c) quote a passage to illustrate their comments. The following excerpts from responses by Monty, Rosa, and Malgorzata illustrate three levels of English language development and ability to structure critical essays about literary pieces.

Monty's carefully structured sentences in Spanish indicate a high level of literacy and ability to analyze the book. Furthermore, his choice of an illustrative sentence (the English quotation) shows that he understoods what he was reading.

Teachers at International High School encourage this first stage of combined use of Spanish and English within meaningful activities. It not only allows students to demonstrate their emerging understandings in their second language by relying on the language they know, but it also provides purposeful opportunities to use meaningful chunks of text in English. By participating in these activities, students begin to appropriate the new language.

Monty

Part I. Brief summary of the book (1-9)

Lo que esta historia nos relata es la vida del pueblo chino desde el año 1865 hasta 1872. En esta época la mujer estaba totalmente discriminada. El libro nos narra la vida de una mujer en particular, Lalu, quien era una muchacha trabajadora, a pesar de las leyes de ese tiempo que decían que las mujeres no podían trabajar.

Despues de eso llegaron los bandidos ...

(Translation: This story is a narrative about the life of the Chinese people from the year 1865 until 1872. At this time women were totally discriminated against. The book tells the story of one of those women, Lalu, a hard working girl in spite of the laws of the time that stated that women could not work.

After this the bandits arrived...)

Part II. Analysis of the theme: The position of women in the economy and society

La posición de la mujer en ese tiempo en la economía: La mujer no juega un papel importante porque mientras el marido trabaja ella espera el dinero para realizar actividades. Ellas no podían trabajar en nada porque en el pueblo chino de antes se decía que el hombre era el que debía mantener el hogar. En ese tiempo el machismo de los hombres de China era tan fuerte que solo les permitían a las mujeres ser amas de casa. En resumen, la mujer no jugó un papel importante en la sociedad.

(Translation: Position of women in the economy at the time: Women did not play an important role because while husbands worked, they had to wait for money in order to perform their activities. They could not work for money because ancient Chinese people believed that it was the man's role to support the home. At that time, the <u>machismo</u> of Chinese men was so strong that women were only allowed to be housewives. To summarize, women did not play an important role in society.)

. . . .

"The farm is my concern, not yours. I will hear no more about it" [McCunn, 1981, p. 17].

Cuando el padre de Lalu usó todo su dinero en esa gran cosecha y lo perdió todo solo por no hacer un alto para escuchar a su hija. El padre de Lalu usó todo su dinero en esa gran cosecha y lo perdió todo por no hacer un alto para escuchar sus consejos. Como resultado, al perder la cosecha y al verse desesperado y sin dinero, decidió vender a su propia hija por solo dos bolsas de semilla.

(Translation: Lalu's father used all of his money in the big harvest and lost it all, just because he did not stop to listen to her advice. As a result, when he lost the harvest and found himself desperate and without money, he decided to sell his own daughter for only two bags of seeds.)

The next piece was written by a student at an intermediate level of proficiency in English. We see in her text a developing sense of English discourse.

Rosa

Part I. This story about the girl life. Her name was Lalu. She live in northern China. They work in farm. Her parents had three children. She was first the daughter. It happened 1880.

When Lalu was young her father try to make good money. He plant winter wheat. He could not successed.

When bandits come Lalus father sold her for two bags of seeds. Her life was distroy. Could she depend some one. Who take care her rest of life. ...?

Chapter 1

"Lalu leaped to her feet... for a moment, she tollered on her little four inch bound feet" [McCunn 1981, 14].

This quote taken from chapter one, from where we come to know that her feet bound to keep in four inch Lalu shaped.

Lalus mother try to help make four inch legs because it was chines tradition. Women could not walk faster than man. When Lalus feet banding she cannot work properly. She leaped her feet when she walk. She was shaking that makes the chickens that pecked and scratched in the dirt around her, sitting them to a loud squaheking.

Women cannot work on the field. Women position less than man. They have to work in the home. They treat the women like a slave. It was bad method. Women have to work in the house and take care the baby.

The women position of economy was not good. They could not do anything whatever they want.

The final excerpt comes from a student who normally would be classified as an advanced ESL student. In it, we see a student comfortable not only with the English language but with the particular genre in which she is writing, a book report. Her sentences are complex, her language is appropriate, and her essay closely follows what is expected of a high school essay. There is still room for development in, for example, the addition of details to make full paragraphs, but she has already appropriated the structure and flow of a school literary essay.

Malgorzata

Part I.

Thousand Pieces of Gold is a novel about the life of a Chinese girl named Lalu. The story begins in the eighties of the nineteenth century in a small village of China.

In the first part of the novel Lalu's father, a poor farmer, lost all the family money taking a great risk—planting winter wheat. As a result Lalu was afraid her father would sell her. She desperately wanted to stay with her family so she convinced her father to let her work on the fields like a man. Her feet were unbinded which was against the Chinese tradition.

After five years, however, a group of bandits came to the town. Lalu's father was forced to sell her, otherwise he might get killed. The family could not survive without him. Lalu was sold for two bags of soybeans.

Lalu was driven by the horde of outlaws. she tried to escape, but she was not successful. In a city she was purchased for an extremely high price by a person who would take her to America.

Part II

One of the most important themes in the book was gold. Gold meant money—in whatever form it was, it was essential for survival. Lalu's life would not be like it was if the financial situation of the family were different.

After Nathoy, Lalu's father, lost the family fortune the neighbors gossiped:

"Her father was going to sell her, . . . for if her father did not pay the land tax, he would be sent to prison and whithout him, the family would starve" [McCunn. 1981, p. 24].

Different kinds of products—in this case, three very different levels of essays, including one written in another language—are accepted in this class because the students have varying degrees of English proficiency. All of the students read the same text and demonstrated—by using their prior knowledge and the help of their peers and teachers—that they understood important ideas in it.

Work Internships

Students at International take a 3-year internship sequence as part of the Personal and Career Development program, which is designed to help them broaden their views of themselves in society and make them aware of options available in the future. It does not prepare them for a specific trade or career, as most vocational programs do. Instead, they take 3 courses (1 each year), combined with an internship (an off-site field experience). During the internship cycle, students spend half of the day 4 days a week at their internship site, then return to school to continue course work for half a day. On the fifth day, they attend a full-day internship seminar (International High School, 1993, p. 123).

The work experience is discussed at school in teams of six students, a teacher, and a couple of student teachers. In these sessions, positive experiences are reflected on to see what can be learned and used from them, and difficult situations are analyzed. Students collaboratively generate possible solutions to their problems and discuss the interventions they have tried. In this way, students learn that by reflecting on their work experiences they can learn a lot, and they also become aware of areas where expectations and behaviors at the work place may be different from those in their home countries.

Work internships are important because they not only smooth the transition from school to work, but they also make school relevant by providing students with real purposes for using English and enabling them to apply the critical skills they have developed in class. Being in New York City helps because of the great variety of internship possibilities the city offers. Students I interviewed were doing their internships in the airline industry (one was interested in becoming a pilot), in hospitals, in schools, and in law offices. Galina, a teacher aide from Russia, had visited the office where two Chinese students were doing their internships. She told me that the girls were "very highly praised" by office personnel and the supervisors. One of the girls had been in the United States for a year and was placed in a public service office. She was "doing very well in face-to-face interactions with the public and learning to operate the switchboard and answer the telephone" (personal communication, May 16, 1995). Recognizing that this second part of the job placed high demands on her developing English proficiency, the agency (in consultation with Galina) had decided that the girl should be on the switchboard for no more than half an hour every day.

Student Teachers

As in many other schools, International provides university students working on their teaching credentials or on Masters degrees the opportunity to conduct their internships in the program. Student teachers at International attend universities such as Columbia, Hunter College, New York University, and The New School for Social Research. Interns at the first three universities spend part of the day at International for part of one semester. Student teachers from The New School for Social Research spend 15 hours a week at International for the first part of the year, observing and becoming acquainted with the system. From February through the end of the high school year (mid June), they spend the whole day. This plan allowed a very special relationship to develop between the teaching staff at International and these teachers in training. Teachers at International are part of the teaching staff at The New School for Social Research, and they teach courses or workshops and supervise their student teachers.

Unlike most other student–teacher arrangements in which a hierarchical relationship exists between a master teacher and the student teacher, the work that takes place between teachers and student teachers at International High school is collaborative and symmetrical. Student teachers work in teams with classroom teachers and share responsibilities: teaching, counseling, meeting in various committees, and contributing to the development of curricula. They do so, not as apprentices, but as members of the community of teachers-as-learners that International fosters. As Charles Glassman commented during one of several conversations,

A lot of the staff development we do has come out of our student teachers. They are taking classes, and they know what is current. I have been teaching for 30 years, and I am not all that current, but these students have a lot of ideas on how to do things. We have found this very valuable. They have moved us.

Glassman's statements were corroborated by several other teachers on different occasions and by my observations during the 3 days I spent at International.

Conclusion

Clearly, International High School has designed an innovative program that breaks with many of the traditional approaches to secondary school education. They have dispensed with the departmental approach to education with their interdisciplinary units and the concomitant collaboration among teachers, including even student teachers' input. They have created exciting theme-based curricula—thus challenging traditional notions about the sequencing of topics and courses—to engage their students and offer them access to a wide range of academic topics. They have made education relevant by linking it directly with a series of work internships that help students learn about postgraduate options in concrete ways. International High School truly demonstrates what can happen when educators move beyond traditional educational approaches and create a program with the needs of immigrant students as its central concern.

One of the lessons I learned from International High School is the strength and cohesion that can occur in smaller schools when there is a vision and the motivation and commitment to work toward it. Everybody who visits International becomes infected with the enthusiasm shared in equal measures by everyone involved. Teachers at International spend incredible amounts of time working together, a process they decided was best. They have scheduled a specific time to collaborate: Every Wednesday morning, while students are involved in extracurricular activities, teachers meet to discuss the issues that concern the running of the school community. But this short time within the working week is only a symbolic recognition of the investment needed to get the school functioning in optimal ways, so they also meet voluntarily before and after school. These meeting times have resulted in an impressive array of ever-changing pedagogical materials and innovative practices. International teachers realize that some teachers, wanting an 8-to-4 job, would not be excited by the prospect of spending hours beyond the "regular" working day to collaborate. International's teachers, however, regard dedication, dialogue, and constant re-examination of practices as not only good for their students but also helpful to them in producing high-quality work and job satisfaction.

Materials Available

- Thematically clustered interdisciplinary units
- Materials on teacher peer review
- Rubrics for assessing students' writing

Contacts

Kathleen Rugger
Aaron Listhaus
International High School at LaGuardia Community College
31-10 Thomson Avenue
Room MB 52
Long Island City NY 11101
Phone (718) 482-5456
Fax (718) 392-6904
E-mail Aaron_Listhaus@cce.org

Harden Middle School, Salinas, California—A Focus on Teacher Professional Development

As schools seek to work effectively with immigrant students, one of the essential pieces in the reform puzzle is how teachers retool themselves to meet the higher academic challenges of changing times and to adjust to changes in the characteristics of their students. Time is essential for teachers to reflect on their everyday practices and to develop collaboratively ways to provide high standards of learning for all of their students, especially for their English language learners. Essential, too, is the facilitation and support of this time-consuming process.

The story of professional development efforts at Harden Middle School exemplifies the challenges faced by many schools seeking to address its teachers' professional development needs, as school staff make a conscious decision to move from more traditional forms of staff development to teacher-directed efforts. Harden's efforts also illustrate how one school, while in the process of resolving internal and societal tensions, focused on making the education of immigrant students the responsibility of the whole school and how difficult such a whole-school process can be. Furthermore, Harden's case shows that professional development can take a long time, can require a great deal of work, and is seldom fully successful. There are no shortcuts available, although there are ways to facilitate and enhance the process.

The Setting

Harden Middle School is a year-round school and one of three middle schools in the Central California city of Salinas, 18 miles from the coast. Although Salinas today has almost 120,000 inhabitants, it still has the feel of a small town, and the old power holders refuse to acknowledge that times are changing. It is precisely this myopia and rejection of change and diversity that Salinas's best-known native John Steinbeck deplored.[5] Salinas also has many of the problems of a big city: high unemployment, juvenile delinquency, and criminal gang activity.

The main economic activity in town is agriculture, which has attracted an immigrant population from Mexico who are employed mostly in fieldwork. Many families follow the harvest cycle, so many of the immigrant students in Salinas are migrants who move from Salinas to Yuma, Arizona, twice a year.

The School and Its Staff

Harden Middle School opened in 1992 in response to population growth in the city and overcrowding at the two existing middle schools. Linda Harris, a recognized instructional leader in the district who had been a teacher and administrator and was principal of a successful alternative high school in town, was chosen to open the school as its principal. Ms. Harris started planning Harden a year before its official dedication. Her many years of holding different positions in the district had given her well-grounded knowledge of the student and teacher population. She was also aware of the challenges the new school would face: low academic standards and low student performance, student transience, a high proportion of English language learners, teachers who taught primarily in traditional transmission-oriented ways, and some teachers who were not enthusiastic about working with immigrant students.

Ms. Harris had a vision for promoting success and high standards in the new middle school in Salinas, but she also knew that unless she started working early with those who would teach at the new school, engaging them in the conversations that would lead to the design of teaching and learning at the school, the sense of ownership and dedi-

---

5. John Steinbeck and the citizens of Salinas had an antagonistic relationship, with city residents refusing to recognize the writer's value, even when he won the Nobel prize for literature. Steinbeck, in turn, when asked if he would like to have a local school named after him, replied that he would rather see a bordello carry his name.

cation that she wanted teachers to have would not be achieved. Because she needed to draw her teachers primarily from those already employed in the district, she conducted several open meetings to inform teachers about the plans for Harden. She invited them to become involved in making major planning decisions and encouraged them to apply to teach at the new site. Some of the best teachers in the district attended these sessions and were involved in curricular discussions, but not all of them wanted to leave their own schools to teach at Harden.

The new middle school was designed around the format of "houses," or schools within a school, called "tracks"[6] at Harden. (This practice is rather common in California's year-round schools.) Groups of students work with a group of teachers and a "learning director." The learning directors serve as counselors and coordinate a guidance program for their respective tracks. The weekly schedule provides 2 hours on Wednesday mornings for teachers to discuss issues related to their tracks before the students arrive. Harden was the first year-round school in Salinas, although individual students do not attend all year; at any one time there are only three tracks in session, while one track is off. During intersession periods, which last 2 weeks, the students can enroll in enrichment programs.

When the school opened, 68% of the students were designated as Limited English Proficient. In order to maximize the efficacy of scarce bilingual teaching personnel, it was decided that students who had no English skills, or whose skills were too limited to enable them to engage in high-level interactions with the mainstream curriculum in English, would be clustered in Track A. Selected to teach this track were the best teachers of English as a second language (ESL) and those who could teach subject matter in Spanish. Students in Track A took their content courses in Spanish and 2 periods a day of ESL. In courses such as art

---

6. In other contexts, the term *track* has connotations of perceived ability levels, differential treatment of students, and self-fulfilling prophecies. At Harden Middle School, it means simply "groups."

and physical education, these students were mainstreamed with their English-speaking peers. Tracks B, C, and D had students with intermediate or full proficiency in English. Their content area classes were either "transitional" (sheltered classes) or "mainstream" (taught exclusively in English).

Professional Growth

The Salinas Union High School District holds 4 or 5 staff development days for all of its teachers throughout the year. Typically, teachers are provided with topic options such as classroom management, collaborative learning, TESA (Teacher Expectations and Student Achievement), critical thinking skills, and so on. They sign up in advance for one topic, which is pursued throughout the year on "strand days." Although attendance at these days is monitored, the level of teacher participation varies, and the benefits of this type of staff development vary significantly.

Being the first year-round school in the district made it possible for Harden to explore new professional development possibilities. Ms. Harris saw the year-round schedule as an opportunity to escape the district staff development format and to design a new format for her school that would more closely mirror what she knew to be effective in teacher professional growth. She was also concerned that since the faculty had little shared history, it was important for them to develop a sense of community.

First year
During the first year of the school's exploration of new professional development options, sessions concentrated on developing teams. Within each of the tracks at Harden, there were two interdisciplinary clusters of teachers called "families." Family teachers needed the time to get to know each other and their students, to discuss and embrace the school's vision, and to plan together. They decided that, given the high number of students with limited English proficiency at the school, professional growth sessions for the second year would concentrate on

preparing all teachers to earn the Language Development Specialist (LDS) certificate. This California certificate, which has since been replaced, was given to credentialed teachers after their ability to work with linguistically diverse students in English had been assessed by means of a test. The equivalent certificate, granted to teachers with bilingual classes, was the Bilingual Certificate of Competence (BCC). The Salinas Union High School District had an interest in LDS certification because in 1986 the district had been found to be noncompliant with state regulations regarding the credentials needed by teachers who worked with second language learners. As a result, it had entered a consent decree through which it had committed itself to providing teachers with the preparation and certification needed to meet the needs of English learners.

Second year

The LDS training at Harden, run by two very capable and knowledgeable teachers at the school who were also state trainers, introduced teachers to the cultural, linguistic, and educational theory on which the education of language minority students in California is based. Teachers discussed the native languages, cultures, and needs of their English language learners; research on language, academic, and conceptual development; and promising instructional practices. The curriculum for the sessions was based on the California Department of Education Bilingual Teacher Training Program (BTTP) modules, designed by bilingual teachers and specialists chosen from around the state to prepare teachers for the LDS certificate. It emphasized specific knowledge about culture and language acquisition and paid less attention to the orchestration of teaching and learning in English for second language learners.

Dissatisfaction with the teacher professional development promoted by the LDS had been widespread throughout the state, and the reaction by Harden teachers was similar to that of other teachers. In fact, to respond to these concerns, the California Commission on Teacher Credentialing replaced the LDS with the Crosscultural, Language, and Academic Development (CLAD) exam by May of 1995. At the same time, the BCC was replaced by the Bilingual Crosscultural, Language, and Academic Development (B-CLAD) certificate. Both new sets of standards and tests focus on generative cultural, linguistic, and pedagogical concepts.

Since Harden teachers and administrators felt that the LDS staff development sessions had not provided the pedagogical knowledge they needed to work with English learners, and the CLAD and B-CLAD guidelines had not yet been published, school staff turned to another area of focus at the California state level: an effort to systematize the knowledge available on sheltered content instruction. The Commission on Teacher Credentialing and the California Department of Education had established a Work Group for Specially Designed Academic Instruction in English (SDAIE) to improve this area of bilingual education (Commission on Teacher Credentialing, 1993). SDAIE is designed to teach challenging academic content in English to English language learners with an intermediate level of proficiency in English. Given the relevance of this methodology, the Harden staff decided to work on SDAIE methodology as the goal for professional growth for the next academic year.

In the meantime, in the summer of 1994, it became evident that a small group of teachers from the nonbilingual tracks at Harden (the mainstream teachers) were dissatisfied with the way instruction had been set up at the school. Their main concern was that so many students in their classes lacked English proficiency. A few teachers felt that placing students in content classes taught in Spanish did not help them learn English and that all students should be mainstreamed into English classes. They also claimed that students in Track A were being segregated because they were deprived of interactions with their English-speaking peers. Some of the students in the school—mostly those in Track A—had been in the United States for several years, and their limited English proficiency was an indication to these teachers that the bilingual programs the students had been part of in the past had not been successful. Paradoxically, at the same time, these teachers indicated that a good number of the students they had in their own tracks were not ready for instruction in English, either.

In response to these concerns, Track A teachers defended the bilingual program, citing the importance of developing higher order academic skills in students' native languages while developing basic proficiency in English and the need to cultivate bilingualism for the benefit of the community and the students. The issue migrated to the community when parents were contacted and mobilized by the teacher group who wanted to change the school program to classes taught exclusively in English. Several parent meetings were held to discuss the value of classes in Spanish, of ESL classes, and sheltered content classes. These meetings were well attended and attracted the attention of the local press. At a time when the U.S. English organization was renewing its campaign of denouncing and discouraging the offering of school services in languages other than English, the local scene mirrored heated arguments about these issues elsewhere in the country.

Clearly, teachers enter the teaching profession with a strong desire to improve their students' present and future possibilities and to improve society as a whole. How these goals are interpreted and realized, however, depends greatly on the levels of personal experience, knowledge, understanding, and reflection of individual teachers. If teachers unquestioningly believe that schools are equalizers in society, they will conclude that the provision of the same program for everybody is critical for equal possibilities to be realized. If, on the other hand, they believe that schools mirror the societies they serve, then they will strive to provide learners with the experiences that will help counterbalance inequities.

Parents want their children to make progress. If they do not know about the importance of developing children's academic skills and content knowledge in a language the children understand, they may follow those they consider to be knowledgeable about the issue. Some of those they consider knowledgeable have told them that ESL courses and instruction in the primary language are a waste of time. Harden needed to solve a major problem: the danger of a fractured teacher force, which could impede the building of consensus in the community within and beyond the school about how to educate English language learners.

The principal's immediate concern was what to do about these controversies and how to frame the discussion within the school in ways that would not lead teachers into negative attacks and counterattacks or pedagogical paralysis. She realized that the new California curricular frameworks presented a view of teaching and learning that emphasized more demanding intellectual tasks and more ambitious student outcomes, a view that most teachers were not familiar with from their own experiences as students in schools and universities. Changing their teaching to meet these new frameworks would not be easy.[7] For teachers to shift teaching paradigms and make pedagogical changes so that all students—native-born and immigrant, fully proficient in English and English language learners—would receive quality education entailed quite a challenge. At the same time, this challenge could provide a common framework within which to begin constructive conversations.

While Ms. Harris considered these issues, she attended a conference organized by the California Association of Bilingual Education (CABE). During that conference, she later told me,

I was listening to Krashen, and at the same time I was thinking about how we could move forward at Harden. The idea became clearer that the whole staff—not just the few who are in charge of teaching the ESL or the transitional (sheltered instruction) teachers, but all teachers—should work with the new standards in mind for all of our students. And all teachers should also be knowledgeable about and responsible for all our students.

---

7. As Lortie (1975) notes, by the time the average student graduates from high school, he or she has spent 13,000 hours in direct contact with classroom teachers. Teachers have normally had 16 years of continuous contact with teachers and professors, in what Lortie calls the apprenticeship-of-observation. Such long-term exposure helps maintain traditional teaching practices in schools.

She decided to convince her planning team—consisting of herself, the learning directors, and a group of teachers—that the whole school should participate in the SDAIE sessions.

Third year

A great deal of planning was devoted to the SDAIE professional growth series. A district mentor teacher, knowledgeable in SDAIE, was asked if she would be interested in conducting it. She was asked to prepare a plan and to meet with the planning committee to discuss it. Although logical, this is not a typical request made of consultants prior to their work with a group of teachers. Several meetings were arranged with the planning committee to develop the best design for teachers' professional growth at the school.

Several concerns needed to be addressed. Everyone wanted to have a body of knowledge presented, experienced, reflected on, and re-created by individual teachers and by groups of teachers working in teams for implementation in class. Some felt that it was no longer necessary to discuss social, cultural, and political issues related to the education of immigrant students. They had learned about those through their LDS training, and raising them again could prove divisive. They felt that the sessions should concentrate on pedagogy. A few teachers, however, felt that such discussions needed to take place, but that they could be embedded in work on pedagogical strategies. This was the strategy that was followed. During the second day of the inservice, for example, in order to model the orchestration of complex reading tasks for English language learners, Harden teachers worked on a jigsaw project in which each of four groups read and discussed a text dealing with the experience of an immigrant student. Each text was about a different student and represented four very different contexts.

The planning committee decided to devote 6 days throughout the year to inservice professional development sessions, with ongoing support mechanisms to ensure that continuous dialog and implementation would take place. Follow-up sessions were designed to provide three different options for teachers with varying degrees of involvement.

These were provided in recognition that some teachers would prefer to embark on a more intense relationship with mentor teachers from the district, some would prefer to work with each other, and still others would prefer involvement in more indirect ways. In this way, every teacher would be accountable for translating into his or her practice some of the ideas discussed in the inservice, but the details would differ, depending on the teacher's prior knowledge and teaching circumstances. During the planning sessions, it was also decided that the overall purpose of the SDAIE series would be to foster the development of a community of practitioners who would engage in constructive interactions to further their understandings of what it means to successfully teach second language learners the challenging content endorsed by the California curricular frameworks.

The three follow-up options were as follows:

1. **Team planning and team teaching for teachers who wanted to be involved more intensively.** The presenter or one of the four resource teachers from the district (who were instructional leaders themselves and attended the inservice sessions) would spend three times a year observing interested teachers, planning a lesson with them, teaching the lesson with them for 2 or 3 days, and discussing the process.

2. **Interactive journal writing.** Between inservice sessions, the teachers who chose this option would (1) describe in a journal an issue they were concerned about in one of their classes and plan one way of addressing it; (2) implement their plan and, as soon as possible, record in the journal a "gut level" reaction to how they felt it had worked; and (3) reflect on the implementation 3 or 4 days later from a more distant perspective. After these three entries had been recorded, the journal would go to the person whom this teacher had chosen to interact with on the team, and this person would write a response.

3. **Peer observation with a colleague.** Guidelines were given for peer observations, and time was provided for those who chose this option

to make pre-observation arrangements, conduct the observation, and have a post-observation conversation.

Federal Title I EIA L.E.P. (Emergency Immigrant Act, Limited English Proficient), Title VII, and Migrant Education funds were used to support the inservice sessions. Title I funds were used to pay for the time of two excellent resource teachers, one a state-recognized language arts and authentic assessment expert, the other a well-respected social studies mentor and teacher. Both spent half of their time at Harden for one year. Their main role was to support teachers in their efforts to adapt their teaching to the needs of their second language learners and to ensure that the language arts program met the state of California Language Arts Framework. At the time, the district had a Title VII grant for math and science to boost the participation of Latino students in advanced math and science courses. The teacher in charge of that program worked with the math and science teachers who requested her support. Finally, a migrant education specialist provided support to the teachers who were teaching classes in students' primary languages.

The three options for follow-up involvement were announced during the first session of the professional growth series, and teachers signed up for their choices. More than half of the teachers signed up for team planning and teaching. As a result of their working together with a team, a more profound type of collaboration was developing. Interactive journals provided another avenue for dialogue about teaching, learning, and school life. The few teachers who chose the peer coaching option reported that it really helped their "families" get to know each other better as teachers and provided an opportunity to see their students in another context.

The SDAIE inservice sessions combined brief presentations, sequences of tasks, and time for teachers to discuss, adapt, and implement some of the presented tasks in their own teaching situations. The sessions presented a view of teaching and learning for immigrant students— and for all students—that was active, interactive, purposeful, and strategic. It was built on Vygotsky's (1978) concept of the Zone of Proximal Development (ZOPD) and Bruner's (1986) concept of observant scaffolding with the gradual handing over of responsibility to students. Through written texts and related activities, the sessions also provided opportunities for teachers to gain insight into the lives of immigrant students in the United States and to consider issues of social and school justice. Teachers said they liked best the time allotted in these sessions for discussion, planning, and adaptation. Some teachers indicated that the "task analysis" done in groups could have been dispensed with, suggesting that it would have been better to spend the time learning about more tasks, rather than analyzing and discussing a few. The following comment comes from one teacher's written evaluation.

I would prefer to spend more time practicing new strategies that I will actually use, rather than discuss the philosophy behind why we use them, although some of what we discussed re-established the reasoning for teaching in the ZPD and scaffolding for second language learners.

Although some teachers would prefer to be handed a package of "tricks" for the classroom, they find that, given opportunities to collaborate and reflect with peers, in time they can move into more proactive roles and creative practices. Unless teachers understand what they are doing, why they are doing it, and under what circumstances tasks may or may not work, it is not possible simply to teach the many ways in which teachers can scaffold instruction for students or structure tasks so that students can scaffold learning for each other.

Near the end of the third year, a change began to take place at Harden. One indication was the teachers' increasing number of pedagogical interactions with each other outside of inservice days and follow-up activities. As one of the Title I resource teachers explained,

I would say there is an emerging culture that focuses on the value of instruction. It is a good thing that everybody is conversant in the same discourse, although there are multiple patterns of participation and growth across time. At lunch time I hear people say, "I tried this with these changes, and this is how it worked," or "As I observed students today engaged in such and such, I thought that something else we could add next time is. . . ." Most of the staff eat lunch together, about 90% of them, which is another manifestation of collaboration, and they talk about teaching. Maybe they do it because this is our role, and when we sit down they say, "We have to start talking about what we are doing in class," but I don't think so. I think they have these conversations anyway.

About the teachers who had been critical of the Harden program, Ms. Harris said,

We have made only a small difference there. With that small group of teachers, we are talking about four teachers, actually three now (one had decided to move to another school the following year), infinitesimal small steps have been taken. I know that one teacher, for example, suddenly saw that there was a reason to group students differently, and that was because she was supposed to scaffold for English learners differently and more intensely at first. That sounds so simplistic, She really thought she was just supposed to try harder with them, and did not really understand that the lesson itself would be different. I thought that was the foundation piece that needed to be there if change was to take place; without that recognition, nothing else could happen.

As minimal as this change appears, it was quite significant because it opened the door for further exploration of ideas. Cindy Lenners, one of the Title I resource teachers who participated in the series and a key facilitator of the follow-up sessions, commented,

One of the teachers I worked with who was very negative about participating in the staff development and having separate classes for language development students has said she is more willing to have discussions on the issue. She will say, "I disagree with that, but I understand there is a need to have real conversations about it." That was a big step for her because at the beginning of the year she didn't even want to discuss anything; she just wanted things her way. And she is using more of the strategies than she ever has in her classes.

Fourth year

Work on SDAIE crystallized for teachers the importance of establishing solid connections across disciplines, and the "family" middle school concept that Harden was implementing was especially conducive to interdisciplinary work. At the end of the third year, the school staff decided that the emphasis of professional development in the fourth year should be on the development of interdisciplinary thematic units. (Three of the four district resource teachers who had provided ongoing support for Harden teachers the previous year were still working part time at Harden in 1995-96.)

This year, the Social Studies Department also participated in a Program Quality Review (PQR) process. As a result of the PQR, all teachers in the Social Studies Department needed to meet several times during the year to analyze how closely the teaching and learning in their department followed the California History and Social Studies framework. The opportunity for self-study provided a tool that made a big difference for the teachers at Harden. In meetings guided by Kelly Smith and Cindy Lenners (two of the resource teachers), teachers arrived at a way of briefly assessing what was going on in their classrooms. In Lenner's words,

One day we were going over some of the essential questions of the PQR and discussing them. We were saying that some of the desired ideas do not happen very often in our classes. Teachers responded, "We do them, I know we do them." I said, "If you do it, there must be some way to show it. You can't say you do it unless there are ways in which you can show it."

Thus, the idea of an evidence check was born. Smith and Lenners produced a chart that highlighted key implementation criteria for the state History and Social Studies Framework. The document, which focused on a student-centered, language-rich approach to teaching and learning, was discussed and adopted by the teachers as a lens for observing each other's classes and for conversing about their observations. It also provided a purpose for visiting each other's classes and refining their ability to observe critically.

During the Fall of 1995, the California Department of Education put out a call for proposals for their Middle School Demonstration grants to schools that were using framework-driven changes successfully. A strong core of teachers suggested that Harden apply. The ideal proposal seemed to be to establish cross-disciplinary teaming between social studies and language arts teachers. All the teachers in these two departments got together to brainstorm ideas for the proposal, which was then written by Smith and Lenners. The school was awarded a 3-year grant of $105,000, 95% of which was to be invested in professional development. Consolidated funds from different sources had already been used for the 4 days that the whole school devoted to interdisciplinary thematic unit planning. The grant enabled the social studies and language arts departments to work on furthering the professional growth of their teachers.

The money was used to buy time for teachers to increase the integration of history, social science, and English language arts; develop curriculum; and enhance their interdisciplinary teaching techniques. Since they received the grant, teachers have met and shared ideas, participated in after-school workshops facilitated by the district resource teachers, and developed interdisciplinary units and authentic assessments. These efforts have enhanced the sense of collegiality among the teachers. In the words of Kelly Smith,

Because of this increased "talk-time," we have begun to develop truly integrated curricula for the language arts and social studies classroom, without losing the integrity of either curricular area.

She also explained how the teachers have been able to create their own models for teaching and learning, by learning from the experience of others but not simply adapting others' ideas:

Some presenters arrived with integration models that worked well in other schools. Some models, however, were not based on the frameworks, or they asked one curricular area to live in service of the other. Though we have included some of their ideas in our integration model, we have now begun to develop our own "model" of integration. ... These inservice sessions and the input from skilled presenters helped us to create our own answers rather than relying on models that were successful for others but not necessarily appropriate for us.

Another important advantage of receiving the grant was that, as a demonstration school, Harden needed to host other teachers from the state who were interested in seeing high-quality teaching of all students within the frameworks. Harden was the first middle school in the state to receive a demonstration grant for interdisciplinary teaching. It was also highly affected by the presence of immigrant students. This situation generated a great deal of interest in the school and created a strong sense of accountability among its teachers.

The evidence check that Harden staff were using became a valuable tool for visitors' observations in Harden's classrooms. As one teacher explained in a written reflection,

As our 80+ guests toured the social studies and language arts classes, student evidence was apparent everywhere. Through the use of student evidence, these visitors and others learn many meaning-making strategies. These include using graphic organizers, simulations, role-playing, symbols and art in the classroom, note-taking, and peer editing. Visitors would see English learners using literature and primary sources in social studies and producing quality reading and writing in language arts. They would see students involved in independent research resulting in the completion of projects and other forms of authentic assessment. Visitors would also learn about many of the resources available to help teach these curricular areas. Through staff development we have become aware of a wide range of teaching strategies to help students develop the academic skills needed for success in all classes.

Other programs at Harden that support professional development

Toward the end of 1995, Harden Middle School teachers decided to join the R.E.A.C.H. Network of Best Classroom Literacy Practices. (R.E.A.C.H. stands for Role of the school community, Effective core literacy program, Appropriate safety net strategies, Continuing professional development, and Home–school partnerships.) This is a group of schools, coordinated by the California Department of Education, that are working on systemic change to foster success with every student in reading and writing across the disciplines. Harden was the first middle school to join the network, which until then consisted only of elementary schools. Harden's teachers were motivated by a desire to establish meaningful communication with the elementary schools that sent students to their school.

As for the school community, Harden already had a Title I literacy project, with three resource teachers, an interdisciplinary team organization that included shared prep periods, Wednesday morning collaboration time, and the Middle School Demonstration grant as the first elements of its program. School staff had also built an effective core literacy program by allotting funds to buy trade books and other materials in Spanish and English for each classroom. In 1994-95, more than $20,000 was devoted for this purpose. Eight thousand dollars was assigned for the purchase of primary sources and other excellent materials; half of that money went to Track A for appropriate Spanish-language materials, of which there had been relatively few. In 1995-96, teachers were each given $200 to enrich their own libraries. All classrooms in the school now have a multitude of books, and on the classroom walls, which are full of student work, one can usually find a corner for "Recommended Books," where students post reviews of their favorites.

Harden also has enrichment classes and a one-on-one after-school tutorial program, staffed by a teacher from each family group, for students who need extra help. The tutorial can be provided in Spanish, English, or in a sheltered mode. Students attend the tutorial for an hour, and a late bus runs for them at the end of the session. In 1995, a reciprocal teaching program was started with adult mentors from the community. Community volunteers are taught how to conduct reciprocal teaching (Brown & Palincsar, 1985) sessions, on a wide variety of texts, with students who are reading below grade level. One of the teachers who was originally negative about Harden's new approaches has organized this program. Companies and businesses provide their employees with time to go to the school to learn the process and volunteer for individual interactions with students. The sessions can take place in English or in Spanish, and their success demonstrates the power of collaborative efforts within and beyond the school. Finally, an Advancement Via Individual Determination (AVID) program (see Lucas, 1997, pp. 209-211) was started in 1995-96 to prepare students for an academic future by mentoring them and providing them with explicit academic skills and individual encouragement.

The home/school partnership component comprises an innovative program called Parent to Parent Training, in which Spanish-speaking parents teach Spanish to English-speaking parents, and English-speaking parents teach English to their Spanish-speaking counterparts. The school also has a Parent Computer Training program, in which students who have developed expertise in their computer class act as instructors in the computer laboratory for parents interested in learning computer skills. Through this program and others, Harden proves that everybody can be the more capable partner in an interaction and can support others' ability to perform at higher levels of competence.

Conclusion

Harden Middle School is a school on the move, with a clear vision of authentic teaching and learning for its whole community of students (including the large immigrant population), teachers, administrators, parents, and the general public. Professional development, which started in more traditional formats and progressed to more collaborative efforts, has enabled teachers to generate creative responses to their situations that are continuously being reformulated and enhanced. With the changing demands placed on teachers by more multilingual and multiethnic student populations, more severe problems of societal disenfranchisement (one just needs to look at the growth of the U.S. prison population), and the increasing need for a citizenry capable of accessing, interpreting, transmitting, and transforming communication, the roles of teachers have expanded beyond what their preservice education prepared them for. This creates a major task for inservice education.

What have we learned about professional development to meet the needs of immigrant students? Some features of optimal professional development are the following:

- It has a clear focus.
- It includes an outside perspective, as for example when teachers work with a "critical friend" from outside the school.
- Collegial professional relationships are developed over time.
- Sustained support for teachers' work is provided.
- Teachers network with like-minded colleagues.

The professional development that has taken place at Harden Middle School is consonant with these principles. Many teachers at the school feel they have increased their understanding of ways to engage their second language learners in meaning-making activities, and they have also discovered that effective approaches can be individualized. The common denominator at the school has been the movement—gradual and different for all teachers—from transmission-oriented to interactive classes. While at first teacher-directed classes dominated the school, increasingly students collaborate with each other, and teachers collaborate with colleagues in their school and from other schools in the state. A visitor to the school will see students, both English speakers and English learners, engaged in posing their own questions and using disciplined inquiry. Students' portfolios, typically kept at the back of classrooms, display students' adventures with language (English and Spanish), with ideas, and with their own creativity. The many ways in which teachers scaffold their students' development of cognitive, linguistic, and academic abilities form the basis for productive collegial conversations.

Sustaining the momentum is difficult, and support for teachers to change needs to be maintained so that the level of exploration and collegiality remains in the service of teachers and second language learners. The first big steps have been taken, for the leadership of the school has clearly communicated to all that the responsibility for educating language learners belongs to everyone in the school. Ideally, the development of teacher capacity at Harden will help teachers defend their English learners and the most appropriate programs for them during difficult times in the future.

Materials Available

- Rubrics for reading competence in English language learners, in English and Spanish
- Portfolio rubrics
- Procedures for Reciprocal Teaching in Spanish and English
- Cross-disciplinary units for World History and Language Arts for 7th and 8th grades
- Bibliography of culturally diverse materials for Language Arts and Social Studies
- Rubrics that can be used as "evidence checks" during brief visits to colleagues' classes

Contacts

Kelly Smith
Cindy Lenners
Harden Middle School
1561 McKinnon
Salinas CA 93906
Phone (831) 796-7300
Fax (831) 796-7305
E-mail clenners@salinas.k12.ca.us
World Wide Web site www.salinas.k12.ca.us

Conclusion and Recommendations

To bring this book to a close, I now circle back to where we began and examine how the four programs profiled in chapter 5 line up with the frameworks and guidelines presented in earlier chapters. As discussed in chapters 1 through 3, immigrant students' education is often negatively affected by sociocultural factors, by misconceptions about their needs, and by the very organization of secondary schools. In many ways, the 10 priorities for effective programs discussed in chapter 4 can help counteract some of these obstacles by creating positive, engaging learning contexts for immigrant students. In their own ways, these four programs have addressed many of the sociocultural and organizational obstacles that their immigrant students face. They have also developed positive learning contexts for these students.

Addressing the Sociocultural Contexts of Immigrant Students' Education

At least three of these programs actively address the sociocultural contexts of their immigrant students' lives, with the exception of Harden Middle School. The Reception Center in Sioux City, Iowa, supports students' families by maintaining contact with them, informing them of their children's educational progress, and referring them to services in the community. Reception Center staff helped to found La Casa Latina, so that Spanish-speaking students and their families could have access to services similar to those already in place for the Vietnamese population the Center serves. In addition, Center staff have chosen to address directly the problems their students have in mainstream schools and in the broader mainstream culture, where their ethnic groups are not always held in high esteem and their immigrant status can lead to negative perceptions.

Calexico High School actively involves the parents of its English language learners in the life of the school by holding all school meetings in Spanish and English and by having a bilingual and bicultural staff to develop and maintain connections between home and school. In many ways, the detracking efforts at Calexico have helped to diminish prejudicial treatment of immigrant students. Without tracking, students have more opportunities to succeed, for they have access to challenging courses and tasks.

At International High School, even though there is little parental involvement, students and teachers regularly discuss the status of immigrant groups in the United States, the kinds of discrimination they face, the negative attitudes about immigrants that have become increasingly common in this country, and the tensions between different "minority" groups, including those that arise between groups of students at International. Such conversations are crucial in this context, where students come from such diverse backgrounds and the potential for intergroup misunderstandings is high. International's internship program also creates valuable connections between school and the realities of work, teaching students through experience far more than they could learn in class what it means to work in the United States.

At Harden, where the focus has been primarily on professional development and improving instruction so that all students can learn, little has yet been done to explicitly address sociocultural factors such as discrimination and negative attitudes toward immigrants. Connections with the community are strong, however, as evidenced by the active involvement of community members in the debate about whether or not teaching content in English is best for learners with little English proficiency. Clearly, school staff and parents are concerned about the children's education, so it is likely that parental involvement will continue to be strong.

Addressing the Structural Obstacles of American Secondary Schools

All four programs have changed their structures to improve the learning opportunities for their immigrant students. They have done this primarily by creating structures that foster cohorts among students and teachers; for example, dividing classes into families at Harden or into interdisciplinary clusters at International. Calexico made restructuring a high priority, and its teachers are working to create smaller institutes to develop stronger bonds between students and their teachers. The Reception Center, as a small and self-contained program with all students learning English together for half a day, also helps build a sense of community among its students and staff. Unfortunately, the separation of this program from the mainstream receiving schools means that this sense of community does not carry over to those schools. Reception Center staff are aware of this problem and work hard to create stronger connections with the mainstream schools. Changes are likely to be long in coming, however, and the mainstream schools are likely to retain the fragmented, departmentalized, and tracked structures that are so common in American secondary schools.

Some of the programs profiled are working to counteract the fragmenting effects of departmentalization by creating interdisciplinary links across content areas. International High School is a premiere example of this kind of approach, with its integrated ESL classes, untracked and unsequenced program, and totally integrated and clustered thematic units. Counseling is done by teachers within the clusters, so that students' academic and personal development are considered together. Calexico High School is also developing interdisciplinary approaches to counteract the fragmenting of knowledge, and Harden's Social Studies and Language Arts departments have done remarkable interdisciplinary and thematic work since they began the process of change several years ago.

The programs that seem to have the most success in organizing in less traditional, more integrated ways are those that have been created specifically for immigrant students, not those that have reformed existing structures. While restructuring traditional schools is quite possible, creating a new program such as International High School or the Reception Center allows the designers to select personnel who share their vision and to design the program in line with that vision. As we have seen at

Harden and Calexico, convincing all of the teachers at a school to re-align themselves with a new vision, and getting all to accept new structures, can be a difficult and extremely time-consuming process.

Addressing the 10 Priorities for Effective Teaching and Learning

To different degrees and in different ways, each of these programs addresses the 10 priorities for effective teaching and learning of immigrant students spelled out in chapter 4. Key personnel (and sometimes almost all personnel) in these programs have learned enough about second language acquisition and the needs of immigrant students that they do not fall prey to the five common misconceptions of how secondary immigrant students should learn (discussed in chapter 2). They do not assume, for example, that students should speak only English, that their conversational English proficiency mirrors their academic proficiency, that language learners' challenges are a result of an inherent lack of motivation, or that all students will learn English at the same rate. Instead, they offer challenging content courses in students' native languages or in sheltered English, they have flexible options for documenting student performance and facilitating student advancement, and they work hard to motivate and engage students.

The extent to which each program actually achieves the goals of each priority varies, depending primarily on the quality and consistency of staff development. Certainly, all four programs work to create communities of learners with respect for all students in their classes and schools (priority 1). They all focus on the cognitive and academic development of their students (priority 2), whether that development comes in the students' native language, through sheltered courses, or in English. They do not water down the content of their courses, but rather work to have high expectations for and high achievement by all students. Naturally, the extent to which high expectations are matched by effective support systems partially determines how successful students will be.

All four programs strive to offer the kind of progressive, experiential, and constructivist instruction described in priorities 3 through 7. Some, like International, have more consistently high levels of such teaching expertise than others, like Harden, where professional development continues. As noted above, professional development is a long and difficult process. Changing instructional paradigms is difficult, especially for teachers who have taught in more traditional ways for decades. However, the success of efforts at Harden and Calexico is heartening, despite the fact that not all of the teachers have achieved the kinds of constructivist, scaffolded teaching that contextualizes tasks and new ideas, introduces concepts cyclically, and makes connections with students' experiences and knowledge.

Creating complex, flexible forms of collaboration (priority 8) and creating opportunities for students to apply their knowledge (priority 9) are both key to the effectiveness of programs like International High School. The senior project at Calexico also offers opportunities to apply knowledge and collaborate, as do many of the activities that take place at the Reception Center. Harden's Social Studies and Language Arts departments, too, have become increasingly more collaborative and applied, both for the students and for their teachers, who are working together to improve the teaching and learning in their departments. At the same time, more can always be done in these areas: The Reception Center faces a major obstacle to increasing collaboration with its separation from the mainstream schools, and the Mathematics and Science departments at Harden have, for the most part, not yet made the kinds of changes that their colleagues in Social Sciences and Language Arts have.

In terms of priority 10, authentic forms of assessment, Calexico and International have instituted new forms of assessment to help their students become more fully engaged in complex tasks, such as Calexico's senior project and the thematically focused research that students at International undertake (such as their research and presentations on religious artifacts). Harden's Social Studies and Language Arts departments have also instituted portfolio assessment systems. The Reception

Center, the mainstream schools it works with, and some departments at Harden, however, still seem to rely on traditional, test-based forms of assessment that do not always accurately indicate immigrant students' abilities or potential.

Addressing Special Student Cases

The four programs seem to be quite effective at helping immigrant students with adequate schooling and proficiency in their native languages to succeed in U.S. schools. Students like Monique, however, with little previous schooling and practically no literacy in her native language, and Carlos, with little academic proficiency in any language, constitute special cases (see chapter 1 for profiles of these two students). While these programs can help such students, they were not designed primarily with their needs in mind. The Reception Center, though especially helpful for students with gaps in their prior schooling, is not prepared for students like Monique. (See Mace-Matluck, Alexander-Kasparik, & Queen, 1998, for profiles of programs that are prepared to serve students with limited prior schooling.) Harden, which has a number of students like Carlos, has not, for the most part, addressed these students' needs explicitly, hoping instead that approaches intended to help other immigrants will also help U.S.-born English learners to develop the proficiencies they need in order to graduate. Students like Monique and Carlos, however, are precisely those who need the most support, for they are the ones who fall through the cracks of systems designed for more traditional immigrants. Even if students like Monique and Carlos are less numerous than other immigrants who have more schooling and more native language proficiency, we do ourselves and our students a disservice if we overlook the needs of these students who are at the highest risk for failure.

Reflections: What Can We Learn From These Programs?

The design of a quality program must be based on the concrete features, possibilities, and constraints that characterize it. At the same time, it is possible to draw some broad generalizations from the experiences of the four programs I studied that will help schools determine their own courses of action. An analysis of the histories and features of these programs indicates the following:

- Providing immigrant students with good programs requires strong leadership at the school site on the part of both teachers and administrators.
- Building a unitary vision for academic change at a school that encompasses both immigrant and non-immigrant students is not an easy process, but it is essential.
- Change in a school takes time and concerted effort.
- Concern about academic preparation for English learners should guide selection of their courses and programs.
- Use of students' first language in classes to provide access to content and to promote engagement is beneficial.
- Effective counseling for immigrant students is critical to their graduation from high school and their pursuit of postsecondary options.
- Programs for immigrant students need to be staffed with adequately prepared teachers who have the vision, understanding, motivation, and ability to engage students in stimulating practices.
- Given their newness to the country and the complexity of their situations, immigrant students need school staff to help them solve problematic situations outside of the school.

In the four programs profiled, talented and dedicated individuals are working to improve the program's design and practice, though the ways they go about doing so vary greatly. Would it be a good idea to promote International High School's design—without doubt the most successful one because it involves all learners, all teachers, and the whole school community in co-constructing achievement for all—as a model to be replicated elsewhere? Certainly not. It has become increasingly clear that the programs most likely to succeed in the education of immigrant students, and all students, involve key actors in serious, grounded analyses of the processes and outcomes at their sites and in conceptualizing together innovations tailored to the concrete realities they face. Every context necessitates a different solution depending on its key features. In fact, International is successful because all of its personnel share vision, understandings, motivation, and the ability to work effectively with immigrant students. They also continually engage in reflection to inform their practice, which has never remained static throughout the school's 10 years.

At other schools, where not all teachers believe equally in the importance of educating immigrant students, or where a culture of reflection and dissatisfaction with the status quo is not the rule, the best programs for immigrant students are those in which they are initially taught by a subset of well-prepared and committed teachers, while administrators and teachers together work to make immigrant students everybody's responsibility. One way to achieve this is to create programs for immigrant populations that are so excellent that they become prestigious. For example, at schools where high-quality academic courses are taught in students' primary languages, these courses could also develop sophisticated skills in the language for those English-speaking students who are studying the language as a foreign language. In this respect, International High School and dual-immersion programs (see Christian, Montone, Lindholm, & Carranza, 1997) have shown us that changes in status of primary language classes are possible when people realize that bilingualism and high educational standards in any language are good for all students, not just for immigrant students.

Recommendations

The recommendations in this section fall into the categories of program development and research.

Program Development

Time, the missing element in the school reform debate, needs to be used in new and better ways for English language learners. We may need to keep schools open longer to meet the needs of children and communities and give teachers the time they need to invest in technology and retraining (National Education Commission on Time and Learning, 1994; Olsen & Jaramillo, in press). As one report suggests, "schools should use some of their resources to extend the school day and year to help LEP students meet their double learning challenge of gaining English proficiency and learning the subject matter" (META, 1995, p. 77). Time changes, for example a switch from traditional to block scheduling, need to be carefully planned and lobbied for with all constituents involved and affected by the change. Otherwise the efforts may fail and contribute to a mistrust in school change.

Oftentimes, immigrant students need to work in the mornings to help their families. Why couldn't some schools have schedules that meet from 3:00 to 10:00 p.m.? This may sound strange in America, but in many foreign countries, secondary schools meet either during the regular schedule from 8:00 a.m. to 3:00 p.m. or in an afternoon/evening arrangement that meets the needs of students who are busy at other times. (See also Mace-Matluck, Alexander-Kasparik, & Queen, 1998, for a description of the Falls Church [VA] High School transitional program.)

Another important and disregarded use of time is summers. Accelerated academies for English language learners could be offered during the summer break that would explore a theme in depth while developing English language learners' conceptual, academic, and linguistic competence.

We also need to create opportunities for adult immigrants to teach courses for adolescent immigrant students in their languages. This could have the dual effect of helping immigrant students develop their skills and bilingualism and of stimulating foreign-born professionals to become recertified in the United States.

We need to stop worrying about the potentially divisive nature of multilingualism in the United States. Immigrants to this country want to speak English very well. In fact, research shows that within the nucleus of the family, English is being learned and family languages are being lost in one or two generations (Wong Fillmore, 1991). The fact that our students are losing the ability to use languages other than English is not only a personal loss, but also a societal waste. Bilingualism needs to be promoted for all American citizens, not just for immigrants (Brecht & Ingold, 1999; Stanford Working Group, 1993).

In addition, we should stop worrying that temporarily separate educational arrangements for particular students represent cases of segregation. Educational designs that separate students are negative only when they condemn them to a lower quality of education. If, as in the case of International High School and the Reception Center, immigrant students learning English are stimulated to achieve their academic and human potential while they develop proficiency in English and enhance their command of their first language, then these students are not being segregated to their detriment, but are rather being educated so that they can be ready to interact with success with native English-speaking peers and contribute much more to the future of this country. On the other hand, immigrant students are segregated *de facto* when they are apparently integrated into a class of English speakers and taught exclusively in English, yet they have no access to the ideas being presented and no way of engaging in the interactions that will make them knowledgeable about the subject.

Research

Research is needed in several areas to better inform the implementation of effective programs for English language learners at the secondary school level. Ethnographic studies of students acquiring English as teenagers could explicate their various daily life experiences that affect their language learning. Questions that might be addressed in such studies include the following:

- How does the differential status (prestige) of students' native languages vis-à-vis English affect English language acquisition?

- How can English proficiency be measured in ways that allow appropriate academic placement in school?
- How can assessment of English language learners combine the use of structured instruments with unstructured, spontaneous speech?
- When is an adolescent English language learner ready to receive unmodified instruction in classes with native English-speaking peers?

Another important area requiring study is professional development for teachers of immigrant students working in various circumstances, including those who have, even unconsciously, anti-immigrant feelings. Several promising avenues of research for teacher growth are already being explored in mainstream education: action research, the use of teaching cases for teacher reflection, and the study of teachers' personal lives. Similar studies should be carried out with teachers who work with linguistically and culturally heterogeneous populations. These studies could then serve as the basis for teacher study groups. Other important topics to be addressed in this area include the following:

- the interaction between specific professional development arrangements (e.g., focused workshops, teacher study groups, whole-school inservice training sessions, and discipline-alike sessions) and goals they may be best suited to;
- how to sustain teacher motivation and prevent high teacher turnover; and
- how to foster collegiality and excellence in difficult heterogeneous teaching and learning environments.

In the area of school and classroom effectiveness for second language learners, research could investigate variability in definitions of effectiveness and how definitions interact with local school and student characteristics. A one-size-fits-all approach is not a valid way to approach the education of English language learners; therefore, we need to know more about the many different ways in which schools can be effective.

The involvement in secondary schools of the families of English language learners is an area in special need of research and development. While many elementary schools reach out to engage students' families, such home–school interaction is far less prevalent in middle schools and high schools. There are many ways in which students can bridge the distance between their families and their schools by researching the community's funds of knowledge. The information gained can be shared, and the resulting collective knowledge can serve as the basis for further knowledge and understandings.

Finally, as a society we need to commit fully to improving the education of the immigrant students in our nation's secondary schools and support that commitment with resources, funding, program and professional development, and serious research endeavors. As the teachers and administrators in the programs profiled in this book have clearly demonstrated, a strong commitment to immigrant students' educational success is ultimately the foundation of all successful programs and instruction. If we support and educate our secondary school immigrant students well, as a society we will gain the future contributions of effective, confident bilingual adults.

References

Abi-Nader, J. (1990). A house for my mother: Motivating Hispanic high school students. *Anthropology & Education Quarterly, 21,* 41-58.

Adger, C., Kalyanpur, M., Peterson, D., & Bridger, T. (1995). *Engaging students: Thinking, talking, cooperating.* Thousand Oaks, CA: Corwin Press.

Ancess, J., & Darling-Hammond, L. (1995). The senior project. Authentic assessment at Hodgson Vocational/Technical High School. In L. Darling-Hammond, J. Ancess, & B. Falk (Eds.), *Authentic assessment in action: Studies of schools and students at work* (pp. 115-167). New York: Teachers College Press.

August, D., & Hakuta, K. (1997). *Improving schooling for language-minority children: A research agenda.* Washington, DC: National Academy Press.

Ball, D., & Rundquist, S. (1993). Collaboration as a context for joining teacher learning with learning about teaching. In D. Cohen, M. McLaughlin, & J. Talbert (Eds.), *Teaching for understanding: Challenges for policy and practice* (pp. 13-42). San Francisco: Jossey-Bass.

Bernstein, B. (1972). Social class, language and socialization. In P.P. Giglioli (Ed.), *Language and social context* (pp. 157-178). New York: Penguin.

Bertolucci, B. (Director), & Thomas, J. (Producer). (1993-94). *Little Buddha.* [Film]. (Available in VHS and DVD format)

Bhachu, P.K. (1985). *Parental educational strategies: The case of Punjabi Sikhs in Britain* (Research Paper 3). Coventry, England: University of Warwick, Centre for Research in Ethnic Relations.

Bialystok, E., & Hakuta, K. (1994). *In other words: The science and psychology of second-language acquisition.* New York: Basic Books.

Brecht, R.D., & Ingold, C.W. (1998). *Tapping a national resource. ERIC Digest.* Washington, DC: ERIC Clearinghouse on Languages and Linguistics. Available: http://www.cal.org/ericcll/digest/brecht01.html

Brown, A., & Palincsar, A. (1985). *Reciprocal teaching of comprehension strategies: A natural history of one program for enhancing learning* (Technical Report No. 334). (Eric Document Reproduction Service No. ED 257 046)

Bruner, J. (1986). *Actual minds, possible worlds.* Cambridge, MA: Harvard University Press.

Calexico High School. (1993). *Introduction to the senior project.* Calexico, CA: Author.

Calexico Unified School District. (1995). *Policies and practices: Towards educational equity.* Calexico, CA: Author.

California Department of Education. (1992). *Second to None: A Vision of the New California High School.* Sacramento, CA: Author.

California State University. (1996). *Undergraduate admission.* Long Beach, CA: Author.

Carter, T.P., & Chatfield, M.L. (1986). Effective bilingual schools: Implications for policy and practice. *American Journal of Education, 95,* 200-234.

Caught in the middle: Educational reform for young adolescents in California public schools. (1993). (Report of the Superintendent's middle grade task force.) Sacramento, CA: California State Department of Education.

Cazden, C. (1988). *Classroom discourse.* Portsmouth, NH: Heinemann.

Chávez, L. (1995, August). One nation, one common language. *Reader's Digest*, pp. 87-91.

Christian, D., Montone, C.L., Lindholm, K.J., & Carranza, I. (1997). *Profiles in two-way immersion education.* McHenry, IL and Washington, DC: Delta Systems and Center for Applied Linguistics.

Cohen, D., McLaughlin, M., & Talbert, J. (Eds.). (1993). *Teaching for understanding: Challenges for policy and practice* (pp. 13-42). San Francisco: Jossey-Bass.

Cohen, E. (1994). Restructuring the classroom: Conditions for productive small groups. *Review of Educational Research, 64,* 1-35.

Collier, V.P. (1995). *Acquiring a second language for school* (Directions in Language Education No. 4). Washington, DC: National Clearinghouse for Bilingual Education. Available: http://www.ncbe.gwu.edu/ncbepubs/directions/04.htm

Commission on Teacher Credentialing, State of California. (1993). *A report on specially designed academic instruction in English (SDAIE).* Sacramento, CA: Author.

Crandall, J.A., Jaramillo, A., Olsen, L., & Peyton, J.K. (in press). Diverse teaching strategies for diverse learners: Immigrant children. In H. Hodges (Ed.), *Educating everybody's children: More teaching stratgies for diverse learners.* Alexandria, VA: Association for Supervision and Curriculum Development.

Crawford, J. (1989). *Bilingual education: History, politics, theory, and practice.* Trenton, NJ: Crane.

Csikszentmihalyi, M., Rathunde, K., & Whalen, S. (1993). *Talented teenagers: The roots of success and failure.* Cambridge, England: Cambridge University Press.

Cummins, J. (1979). Cognitive/academic language proficiency, linguistic interdependence, the optimum age question and some other matters. *Working Papers on Bilingualism, 19,* 121-129.

Cummins, J. (1981). The role of primary language development in promoting educational success for language minority students. In California State Department of Education, Office of Bilingual Bicultural Education (Ed.), *Schooling and language minority students: A theoretical framework* (pp. 3-49). Los Angeles: California State University; Evaluation, Dissemination and Assessment Center.

Darder, A. (1991). *Culture and power in the classroom: A critical foundation for bicultural education.* New York: Bergin & Garvin.

Deci, E.L. (1995). *Why we do what we do: The dynamics of personal autonomy.* New York: G.P. Putnam's Sons.

Deci, E.L., & Ryan, R.M. (1985). *Intrinsic motivation and self-determination in human behavior.* New York: Plenum Press.

Delpit, L. (1995). *Other people's children: Cultural conflict in the classroom.* New York: The New Press.

Dixon, C., & Nessel, D. (1983). *Language experience approach to reading (and writing) for second language learners.* Hayward, CA: The Alemany Press.

Doggett, G. (1994). *Eight approaches to language teaching. ERIC Digest.* Washington, DC: ERIC Clearinghouse on Languages and Linguistics. Available: http://www.cal.org/ericcll/

Ellis, R. (1994). *The study of second language acquisition.* Oxford, England: Oxford University Press.

Elmore, R. (1995, December). Structural reform and educational practice. *Educational Researcher, 24*(9).

Espenshade, T.J. (Ed.). (1997). *Keys to successful immigration: Implications of the New Jersey experience.* Washington, DC: The Urban Institute Press.

Fairclough, N. (1989). *Critical language awareness.* Harlow, England: Longman.

Fairclough, N. (1993). *Language and power* (6th impression). Harlow, England: Longman.

Faltis, C. (1993). *Jointfostering: Adapting teaching strategies for the multilingual classroom.* New York: Merrill.

Ferreiro, E., Pellicer, A., Rodríguez, B., Silva, A., & Vernon, S. (1991). *Haceres, quehaceres y deshaceres con la lengua escrita en la escuela rural.* México D.F.: Departamento de Investigaciones Educativas del Centro de Investigación y Estudios Avanzados (Instituto Politécnico Nacional).

Foley, D.E. (1991). Reconsidering anthropological explanations of ethnic school failure. *Anthropology & Education Quarterly, 22,* 60-86.

Freire, P., & Macedo, D. (1987). *Literacy: Reading the word and the world.* South Hadley, MA: Bergin & Garvey.

Gándara, P. (1995). *Choosing higher education: Antecedents to successful educational outcomes for low income Mexican students.* Albany, NY: SUNY Press.

García, E. (1992). Effective instruction for language minority students: The teacher. *Journal of Education, 173,* 130-141.

García, E. (1994). *Understanding and meeting the challenge of student cultural diversity.* Boston: Houghton Mifflin.

García, E. (1996). Preparing instructional professionals for linguistically and culturally diverse students. In J. Sikula, T. Buttery, & E. Guyton (Eds.), *Handbook of research on teacher education* (pp. 802-813). New York: Simon & Schuster Macmillan.

Gardner, H. (1989). *To open minds: Chinese clues to the dilemma of contemporary education.* New York: Basic Books.

Gardner, H. (1991). *The unschooled mind: How children learn, and how schools should teach.* New York: Basic Books.

Gardner, R.C., & Tremblay, P.F. (1994). On motivation, research agendas, and theoretical frameworks. *The Modern Language Journal, 78,* 359-368.

Gibson, M. (1993). The school performance of immigrant minorities: A comparative view. In E. Jacob & C. Jordan (Eds.), *Minority education: Anthropological perspectives* (pp. 113-118). Norwood, NJ: Ablex.

Gibson, M. (1995). Additive acculturation as a strategy for school improvement. In R. Rumbaut & A. Cornelius, *California's immigrant children: Theory, research, and implications for educational policy* (pp. 77-105). San Diego, CA: University of California, Center for U.S.–Mexican Studies.

Goldenberg, C. (1991). *Instructional conversations and their classroom application* (Educational Practice Report No. 2). Santa Cruz, CA and Washington, DC: National Center for Research on Cultural Diversity and Second Language Learning.

González, J.M., & Darling-Hammond, L. (1997). *New concepts for new challenges: Professional development for teachers of immigrant youth.* McHenry, IL and Washington, DC: Delta Systems and Center for Applied Linguistics.

Goodman, Y. (1978). Kid watching: An alternative to testing. *National Elementary School Principal, 57,* 41-45.

Hakuta, K. (1986). *Mirror of language.* New York: Basic Books

Hakuta, K., & D'Andrea, D. (1992). Some properties of bilingual maintenance and loss in Mexican background high school students. *Applied Linguistics, 13,* 72-99.

Hargreaves, A. (1994). *Changing teachers, changing times: Teachers' work and culture in the postmodern age.* New York: Teachers College Press.

Harklau, L. (1994). Tracking and linguistic minority students: Consequences of ability grouping for second language learners. *Linguistics and Education, 6,* pp. 217-244.

Heath, S.B. (1983). *Ways with words.* Cambridge, England: Cambridge University Press.

Heath, S.B. (1986). Sociocultural contexts of language development. In *Beyond language: Social and cultural factors in schooling language minority students.* Los Angeles: California State University; Evaluation, Dissemination and Assessment Center.

Heath, S.B., & McLaughlin, M.W. (Eds.). (1993). *Identity & inner-city youth: Beyond ethnicity and gender.* New York: Teachers College Press.

Herrnstein, R., & Murray, C. (1994). *The bell curve: Intelligence and class structure in American life.* New York: The Free Press.

Higgs, T.V., & Clifford, R. (1982). The push toward communication. In T.V. Higgs (Ed.), *Curriculum, competence, and the foreign language teacher* (pp. 51-79). Lincolnwood, IL: National Textbook Company.

Hinton, S.E. (1967). *The Outsiders.* New York: Dell.

International High School at LaGuardia Community College. (1993). *Project PROPEL handbook: Resources for adopting sites.* Long Island City, NY: Author.

International Schools Partnership (International High School at LaGuardia Community College, Manhattan International High School, and Brooklyn International High School). (n.d.). *Twenty-first century schools: A five year plan submitted by The International Schools Partnership.* Long Island City, NY: International High School.

Jensen, A.R. (1969). How much can we boost I.Q. and scholastic achievement? *Harvard Educational Review, 39,* 1-123.

Johnson, S.M. (1990). The primacy and potential of high school departments. In M. McLaughlin, J. Talbert, & N. Bascia (Eds.), *The contexts of teaching in secondary schools: Teachers' realities.* New York: Teachers College Press.

Kagan, S., & McGroarty, M. (1993).Principles of cooperative learning for language and content gains. In D.D. Holt (Ed.), *Cooperative learning: A response to linguistic and cultural diversity* (pp. 47-66) McHenry, IL and Washington, DC: Delta Systems and Center for Applied Linguistics.

Kamin, L.J. (1974). *The science and politics of I.Q.* New York: John Wiley & Sons.

Kaplan, R.B. (1988). Contrastive rhetoric and second language learning: Notes toward a theory of contrastive rhetoric. In A.C. Purus (Ed.), *Writing across languages and cultures: Issues in contrastive rhetoric.* Beverly Hills, CA: Sage.

Kashin, M. (1988). The Soviet Union. In T.N. Postlethwaite (Ed.), *Encyclopedia of comparative education and national systems of education.* Oxford and New York: Pergamon Press.

Katz Weinberg, S. (1994, October). *Where the streets cross the classroom: A study of Latino students' perspectives on cultural identity in city schools and neighborhood gangs.* Paper presented at the Language Minority Research Institute Conference on Education and Immigration, University of California, Riverside.

Kohn, A. (1993). *Punished by rewards: The trouble with gold stars, incentive plans, A's, praise and other bribes.* New York: Houghton Mifflin.

Krashen, S. 1985. *The input hypothesis: Issues and implications.* London: Longman.

Lambert, W.E., & Cazabon, M. (1994). *Students' views of the Amigos program* (Research Report No. 11). Santa Cruz, CA and Washington, DC: National Center for Research on Cultural Diversity and Second Language Learning.

Lortie, D.C. (1975). *Schoolteacher: A sociological study.* Chicago: University of Chicago Press.

Lucas, T. (1993). *Applying elements of effective secondary schooling for language minority students: A tool for reflection and stimulus to change* (Program Information Guide No. 14). Washington, DC: National Clearinghouse for Bilingual Education. Available: http://www.ncbe.gwu.edu/ncbepubs/pigs/pig14.htm

Lucas, T. (1997). *Into, through, and beyond secondary school: Critical transitions for immigrant youths.* McHenry, IL and Washington, DC: Delta Systems and Center for Applied Linguistics.

Lucas, T., Henze, R., & Donato, R. (1990). Promoting the success of Latino language-minority students: An exploratory study of six high schools. *Harvard Educational Review, 60,* 315-340.

Mace-Matluck, B.J., Alexander-Kasparik, R., & Queen, R.M. (1998). *Through the golden door: Educational approaches for immigrant adolescents with limited schooling.* McHenry, IL and Washington, DC: Delta Systems and Center for Applied Linguistics.

Matute-Bianchi, M.E. (1991). Situational ethnicity and patterns of school performance among immigrant and nonimmigrant Mexican-descent students. In M. Gibson & J. Ogbu (Eds.), *Minority status and schooling: A comparative study of immigrant and voluntary minorities.* New York: Garland.

McCunn, R.L. (1981). *A thousand pieces of gold: A biographical novel.* New York: Beacon Press.

McDonnell, L.M., & Hill, P. T. (1993). *Newcomers in American schools: Meeting the educational needs of immigrant youth.* Santa Monica, CA: Rand.

McLaughlin, B. (1992). *Myths and misconceptions about second language learning: What every teacher needs to unlearn* (Educational Practice Report No. 5). Santa Cruz, CA and Washington, DC: National Center for Research on Cultural Diversity and Second Language Learning.

McLaughlin, M., Irby, M., & Langman, J. (1994). *Urban sanctuaries: Neighborhood organizations in the lives and futures of inner-city youths.* San Francisco: Jossey-Bass.

McLaughlin, M., & Shepard, L. (1995). *Improving education through standards-based reform.* Stanford, CA: The National Academy of Education.

McLaughlin, M., & Talbert, J. (1990). The contexts in question: The secondary school workplace. In M. McLaughlin, J. Talbert, & N. Bascia (Eds.), *The contexts of teaching in secondary schools: Teachers' realities.* New York: Teachers College Press.

Mehan, H., Hubbard, L., Lintz, A., & Villanueva, I. (1994). *Tracking untracking: The consequences of placing low track students in high track classes* (Research Report No. 10). Santa Cruz, CA and Washington, DC: National Center for Research on Cultural Diversity and Second Language Learning.

Minicucci, C., & Olsen, L. (1992). *Programs for secondary Limited English Proficient students: A California study* (Occasional Papers in Bilingual Education No. 5). Washington, DC: National Clearinghouse for Bilingual Education.

Moll, L., & Díaz, S. (1993). Change as the goal of educational research. *Anthropology and Education Quarterly, 18,* 300-334.

Multicultural Education, Training, and Advocacy, Inc. (1995). *Programs for limited English proficient students in 15 California secondary schools.* Sacramento, CA: Author.

Muncey, D., & McQuillan, P. (1993). Preliminary findings from a five-year study of the Coalition of Essential Schools. *Phi Delta Kappan,* 186-189.

National Center for Children in Poverty. (1998, March). *Young children in poverty: A statistical update.* Available: http://cpmcnet.columbia.edu/dept/nccp/98uptext.html

National Education Commission on Time and Learning. (1994, September). *Prisoners of time: Schools and programs making time work for students and teachers.* Washington, DC: U.S. Government Printing Office.

Neumann, R.A. (1996). Reducing Hispanic dropout: A case of success. *Educational Policy, 10*(1), 22-45.

Oakes, J. (1985). *Keeping track: How schools structure inequality.* New Haven: Yale University Press.

Ogbu, J.U. (1978). *Minority education and caste: The American system in cross-cultural perspective.* New York: Academic Press.

Ogbu, J.U. (1991). Immigrant and involuntary minorities in comparative perspective. In M.A. Gibson & J.U. (Eds.), Ogbu, *Minority status and schooling: A comparative study of immigrant and voluntary minorities* (pp. 3-33). New York: Garland.

Ogbu, J.U., & Matute-Bianchi, M.E. (1986). Understanding sociocultural factors: Knowledge, identity, and school adjustment. In *Beyond language: Social and cultural factors in schooling language minority students* (pp. 73-142). Sacramento, CA: California State Department of Education, Bilingual Education Office.

Olsen, L. (1995). School restructuring and the needs of immigrant students. In R. Rumbault & W.A. Cornelius (Eds.), *California's immigrant children: Theory, research, and implications for educational policy.* San Diego, CA: University of California, Center for U.S.–Mexican Studies.

Olsen, L., & Dowell, C. (1989). *Bridges: Promising programs for the education of immigrant children.* San Francisco: California Tomorrow.

Olsen, L., & Jaramillo, A. (in press). When time is on our side: Redesigning schools to meet the needs of immigrant students. In P. Gándara (Ed.), *The dimension of time and the challenge of school reform.* New York: SUNY Press.

O'Malley, J.M., & Chamot, A.U. (1989). *Learning strategies in second language acquisition.* Cambridge, England: Cambridge University Press.

Oxford, R. (1990). *Language learning strategies: What every teacher should know.* New York: Newbury Press.

Palincsar, A., David, I., & Brown, A. (1992). Using reciprocal teaching in the classroom: A guide for teachers. Unpublished manuscript, The Brown/Campione Research Group.

Pease-Alvarez, L., Espinosa, P., & García, E. (1991). Effective instruction for language minority students: An early childhood case study. *Early Childhood Research Quarterly, 6,* 347-363.

Pease-Alvarez, L., & Hakuta, K. (1993). Perspectives on language maintenance and shift in Mexican-origin students. In P. Phelan & A.L. Davidson (Eds.), *Renegotiating cultural diversity in American schools.* New York: Teachers College Press.

Perkins, D. (1993). *An apple for education: Teaching and learning for understanding* (EdPress Elam Lecture, Rowan College of New Jersey). Glasboro, NJ: EdPress.

Peterson, S. (1993, July 22). Testimony of Sally Peterson, President of Learning English Advocates Drive. *Bilingual Education: Hearing before the Subcommittee on Elementary, Secondary, and Vocational Education, of the House Committee on Education and Labor,* 103rd Cong., 1st Sess.

Phelan, P., Davidson, A., & Cao, H. (1991). Students' multiple worlds: Negotiating the boundaries of family, peer, and school cultures. *Anthropology and Education Quarterly, 22.*

Ramírez, J.D., & Merino, B. J. (1990). Classroom talk in English immersion, early-exit and late-exit transitional bilingual education programs. In R. Jacobson & C. Faltis (Eds.), *Language distribution issues in bilingual schooling* (pp. 61-103). Clevedon, England: Multilingual Matters.

Ramírez, D., Yuen, S., Ramey, D., & Pasta, D. (1991). *Final report: Longitudinal study of immersion strategy, early-exit and late-exit transitional bilingual education programs for language-minority children.* San Mateo, CA: Aguirre International.

Reyes, M. (1992). Challenging venerable assumptions: Literacy instruction for linguistically different students. *Harvard Educational Review, 62,* 427-446.

Richardson, L. (1993, December 28). Thriving on difference: International High students speak language of learning. *The New York Times,* pp. B1, B4.

Rodríguez, L.J. (1993). *Always running—La vida loca: Gang days in L.A.* New York: Touchstone.

Rodríguez, R. (1982). *Hunger of memory: The education of Richard Rodríguez, an autobiography.* Toronto: Bantam Books.

Roth, T. (1995, October). The MacNeil/Lehrer news hour: Debate on the officialization of English. New York and Washington, DC: Public Broadcasting Service.

Rubin, J. (1975). What the "good language learner" can teach us. *TESOL Quarterly, 9,* 41-51.

Rubin, J., & Thompson, I. (1982). *How to be a more successful language learner.* Boston, MA: Heinle & Heinle.

Santiago, E. (1994). *When I was Puerto Rican.* New York: Vintage Books.

School expects, gets excellence. (1993, December 20). *The Phoenix Gazette.*

Schwab, J.J. (1964). The structure of disciplines: Meanings and significance. In G. W. Ford & L. Pugno (Eds.), *The structure of knowledge and the curriculum.* Chicago: Rand McNally.

Shulman, L. (1995). *Fostering communities of teachers as learners* (Report to the Andrew W. Mellon Foundation). Unpublished manuscript, Stanford University.

Simon, L.A. (Director), & Trench, T. (Executive Producer). (1997). *P.O.V.: Fear and learning at Hoover Elementary* [Film].

Skehan, P. (1989). *Individual differences in second-language learning.* London: Edward Arnold.

Skutnabb-Kangas, T. (1981). *Bilingualism or not: The education of minorities.* Clevedon, England: Multilingual Matters.

Spindler, G., & Spindler, L. (1993). The processes of culture and person: Cultural therapy and culturally diverse schools. In P. Phelan & A.L. Davidson (Eds.), *Renegotiating cultural diversity in American schools* (pp. 27-51). New York: Teachers College Press.

Stanford Working Group. (1993). *Federal education programs for Limited English Proficient students: A blueprint for the second generation.* Stanford, CA: Stanford University.

Suárez-Orozco, M. (1989). *Central American refugees and U.S. high schools: A psychosocial study of motivation and achievement.* Stanford, CA: Stanford University Press.

Suárez-Orozco, M. (1996). "Becoming somebody": Central American immigrants in U.S. inner-city schools. In E. Jacob & C. Jordan (Eds.), *Minority education: Anthropological perspectives* (pp. 129-143). Norwood, NJ: Ablex.

Suzuki, B. (1983). The education of Asian and Pacific Americans: An introductory overview. In D. Nakanishi & M. Hirono-Nakanishi (Eds.), *The education of Asian and Pacific Americans: Historical perspectives and prescriptions for the future.* Phoenix, AZ: Oryx Press.

Taylor, M.L. (1993). The language experience approach. In J.A. Crandall & J.K. Peyton (Eds.), *Approaches to adult ESL literacy instruction* (pp. 47-58). McHenry, IL and Washington, DC: Delta Systems and Center for Applied Linguistics.

Tharp, R., & Gallimore, R. (1988). *Rousing minds to life: Teaching, learning and schooling in social context.* Cambridge, England: Cambridge University Press.

Trueba, H.T. (1991). Comments on Foley's "Reconsidering anthropological explanations...." *Anthropology & Education Quarterly, 22,* 87-94.

Tuan, M. (1995). Korean and Russian students in a Los Angeles high school: Exploring the alternative strategies of two high-achieving groups. In R. Rumbaut & W. Cornelius (Eds.), *California's immigrant children: Theory, research, and implications for educational policy.* San Diego, CA: University of California, Center for U.S.-Mexican Studies.

Twitching, J. (Producer). (1993). *Mosaic: Children without prejudice.* [Video]. Part of the BBC-produced series, *Save the children: Early years anti-racist training.*

University of California. (1996). *Introducing the University.* Oakland, CA: Student Academic Services.

van Lier, L. (1995). *Introducing language awareness.* London: Penguin.

Veldman, C. (1983). *Language shift in the United States.* Berlin: Mouton.

Vigil, J.D. (1988). *Barrio gangs: Street life and identity in Southern California.* Austin, TX: University of Texas Press.

Vigil, J.D. (1993). Gangs, social control, and ethnicity: Ways to redirect. In S.B. Heath & M.W. McLaughlin (Eds.), *Identity and inner-city youth: Beyond ethnicity and gender* (pp. 94-119). New York: Teachers College Press.

Vygotsky, L. (1978). *Mind in society.* Boston: Harvard University Press.

Walqui, A. (1997). *The development of teachers' understanding: Inservice professional growth for teachers of English language learners.* Unpublished doctoral dissertation, Stanford University, Stanford, California.

Wiley, T.G. 1996. *Literacy and language diversity in the United States.* McHenry, IL and Washington, DC: Delta Systems and Center for Applied Linguistics.

Wong, M. (1980). Model students? Teachers' perceptions and expectations of their Asian and white students. *Sociology of Education, 53,* 236-246.

Wong, S. (1987). The language learning situation of Asian immigrant students in the U.S.: A socio- and psycholinguistic perspective. *NABE Journal, 11,* 203-234.

Wong Fillmore, L. (1991). When learning a second language means losing the first. *Early Childhood Research Quarterly, 6*(3), 323-346.

How to order titles from ERIC

Citations with ED numbers are documents from *Resources in Education.* They can be read at a library with an ERIC microfiche collection or purchased, in microfiche or paper copy, from ERIC Document Reproduction Service (EDRS), 7420 Fullerton Rd Suite 110, Springfield VA 22153-2852 (Phone: 800-443-3742) (E-mail: service@edrs.com) (World Wide Web: www.edrs.com).

For the location of the nearest ERIC collection, contact the ERIC Clearinghouse on Languages and Linguistics (ERIC/CLL), 4646 40th St NW, Washington DC 20016-1859 (Phone: 800-276-9834) (Fax: 202-363-7204) (E-mail: eric@cal.org).

Index